W9-BZO-794

# PHARMACY LAW SUMMARY FOR CPJE®

## 2018 EDITION

PAMELA TU, PHARMD
KAREN SHAPIRO, PHARMD, BCPS

RXPREP, INC.

**PRIMARY SOURCES**
California Lawbook for Pharmacy, at http://www.pharmacy.ca.gov/laws_regs/lawbook.pdf

**CPJE Candidate Information Bulletin**

*The Script* Newsletters, at http://www.pharmacy.ca.gov/publications/script.shtml

DEA's *Pharmacist's Manual*, at www.deadiversion.usdoj.gov/pubs/manuals/pharm2/

Food and Drug Administration, at www.fda.gov

VERSION 2.1

Cover Design by Shannon Zinda

Book Design by MidnightBookFactory.com

## PREFACE

Welcome to RxPrep's California Practice Standards and Jurisprudence Examination for Pharmacists (CPJE) exam review.

This manual is intended to be used with RxPrep's CPJE online video and test bank course. The video segments and test bank sections correlate with the topics in this manual. The course is intended to be used in this manner:

- While watching the video segment, highlight the material in the manual that you need to review.

- Study the highlighted areas.

- Test yourself with the corresponding test bank section. Each test bank question should be known prior to testing, with an understanding of why the answer is correct. This will permit correct responses to similar items, worded differently, that you may find on the actual exam.

Please visit the RxPrep website to find a study method that has worked well for many other CPJE test takers.[1] To perform well on the CPJE, the score on the NAPLEX exam should have been high. If this was not achieved, please consider using the NAPLEX program with the CPJE program. The NAPLEX course includes the topics that overlap in both exams. There will be a majority of drug-related questions on the CPJE. This course covers the items not included with the NAPLEX course (such as therapeutic interchange, formulary management, physical assessments, health screenings, and medication utilization evaluation), along with the California pharmacy law, in detail.

The CPJE test banks include advanced drug monitoring questions and common drugs that are interchanged in the hospital setting. These questions are quite important for those that have practiced primarily in the community setting. Help is included with this course; email instructors@rxprep.com if stuck on a concept or question.

If RxPrep has prepared updates on this material, it will be posted with your CPJE online access and can be printed out when logged into your account from an Internet browser. There will be an announcement posted on the website or sent to your RxPrep mobile application on your phone or tablet when there is a new update.

We wish you the best for your CPJE preparation.

The RxPrep Team
www.rxprep.com

---

1   https://rxprep.com/resources/25 (accessed 2018 Feb 17).

# TABLE OF CONTENTS

# Introduction

## CALIFORNIA PHARMACY JURISPRUDENCE EXAM

The California Practice Standards and Jurisprudence Examination for Pharmacists (CPJE) is one of two exams a candidate must pass in order to be a California-registered pharmacist. The other exam is the North American Pharmacist Licensure Examination (NAPLEX), which is administered by the National Association of Boards of Pharmacy. For more information on the pharmacist application process, visit the California Board of Pharmacy website.[2] Although the CPJE is a law exam, a vast majority of the questions are clinical in nature. Students with a NAPLEX score in the triple digits generally feel comfortable with the clinical content of the CPJE. It is recommended to allocate more time reviewing clinical topics for students who passed the NAPLEX by a relatively lower margin.

Pharmacy law is constantly evolving to protect patients, keep up with the expanding scope of pharmacy practice, and address advances in healthcare technology. Before sitting for the exam, check the California Board of Pharmacy website for updates on pharmacy law. If Rx-Prep has prepared updates on this material, it will be posted with your CPJE online access and can be printed out when logged into your account from a web browser.

Review the CPJE candidate information bulletin for information on exam logistics, exam content, and practice questions.[3] The CPJE covers the following three areas: patient medications, patient outcomes, and pharmacy operations. The RxPrep California Law Summary for CPJE is a comprehensive and concise resource specifically tailored towards preparing for the law portion of the CPJE and should be used with the RxPrep NAPLEX course. The RxPrep CPJE Course also covers the clinical topics that are not covered in the RxPrep NAPLEX course (e.g., several pharmacist-provided clinical services authorized under SB 493, drug formularies, therapeutic interchange, standard order sets, and medication utilization evaluation). RxPrep recommends taking the CPJE no later than 2 weeks after the NAPLEX in order to retain the drug information you reviewed for the NAPLEX. However, some students will take the CPJE first due to scheduling conflicts, and this is often fine.

2   http://www.pharmacy.ca.gov/applicants/rph.shtml (accessed 2018 Feb 16).
3   http://www.pharmacy.ca.gov/publications/phy_handbook_psi.pdf (accessed 2018 Feb 16).

Any information in RxPrep's NAPLEX course can be tested on the CPJE, including calculations, such as flow rates, renal clearance calculations and compounding calculations. Information in these chapters may also be important: Infectious Disease, HIV, Immunizations, Medication Safety & Quality Improvement, Critical Care & Fluids/Electrolytes, and IV Drug Compatibility, Stability, Administration & Degradation. The RxPrep NAPLEX test bank called *Indications* should be reviewed.

## SUPPLEMENTAL RESOURCES

The CPJE Candidate Information Bulletin recommends preparing for the exam with these sources:

- The California Pharmacy Law Book, which includes pharmacy-related regulations from the Business and Profession Code (B&PC), California Code of Regulations (CCR), and Health and Safety Code (H&SC).[4] In the RxPrep CPJE manual, key regulations are referenced for the applicant who wishes to look them up in the Law Book. For example, the information on pharmacists-in-charge discussed in this manual references CCR 1709.1, which refers to the California Code and Regulations, Section 1709.1.

- Previous issues of the board's newsletter, *The Script*.

- Published monographs on drug therapy, *Health Notes* (this publication has not been issued for the past several years).

- Community Pharmacy and Hospital Outpatient Pharmacy Self-Assessment form.

Additionally, reviewing the Compounding Self-Assessment form is helpful for the exam. The self-assessment forms are completed by the pharmacist-in-charge for every California-licensed pharmacy, by July 1st of each odd-numbered year. The self-assessment forms are developed by the California Board of Pharmacy as a tool for the pharmacist-in-charge to ensure that the pharmacy is following all the legal requirements for operations. Each item is reviewed in this course and is tested in the CPJE test banks.

---

4   http://www.pharmacy.ca.gov/laws_regs/lawbook.pdf (accessed 2018 Jan 2).

## STUDY TIPS

Use your time wisely and create a study plan.[5] Use it to your advantage if you are currently on rotations or working in a pharmacy setting with direct patient care. When you are handling drugs, look at the brand and generic and think of the indication. Practice reviewing the patient profile and decide if this is a safe and appropriate drug for the patient. Pretend that you are the pharmacist-in-charge and complete the pharmacy self-assessment form.[6]

Adult learners do not learn well passively, by sitting in front of a text or computer screen. Simply reading and highlighting a chapter may not be sufficient. Active learning strategies (like making notecards, making your own written summaries and explaining concepts out loud) tend to work well for adult learners.

## CPJE TEST DESIGN

The CPJE is a 2-hour exam with 90 multiple-choice questions. Of the 90 questions, 75 questions count towards the score. The other 15 questions are pretest questions and do not count. The board uses the pretest questions to determine if they are appropriate for use in future exams. These are dispersed throughout the test and there is no way to tell if a specific question will be counted. It is not possible to change an answer once the answer choice is confirmed and you have moved to the next question. There is only one answer for each question. Since scores on the examination are based on the number of correct answers, there is no penalty for guessing. It is to your advantage to answer every question. About 30 days after you take the CPJE examination, the board will mail your score to your address. Results will not be given over the telephone or through email.

The board occasionally conducts a quality assurance (QA) assessment to ensure that the exam questions are appropriate. Anyone testing during a QA will need to wait until 400 candidates test during that time, and the results of the exams are reviewed.

## CPJE DETAILED CONTENT OUTLINE

The revised CPJE Candidate Information Bulletin Content Outline became effective on April 1, 2016.[7] A majority of the items on the previous outline are included, plus these items: Administering medications, biologics and immunizations, compounding, pharmacokinetic (PK) calculations, using drug literature, furnishing drugs, performing physical assessments and health screenings, preparing for emergencies, and promoting public health.

5   https://rxprep.com/resources/25 (accessed 2018 Feb 17).
6   http://www.pharmacy.ca.gov/licensees/facility/self_assess.shtml (accessed 2018 Feb 16).
7   http://www.pharmacy.ca.gov/forms/exam_outline_after0416.pdf (accessed 2018 Feb 16).

# California Board of Pharmacy
# Detailed Content Outline

## 1. PATIENT MEDICATIONS                                    20 items

### A. Collect, Organize, and Evaluate Information

1. Obtain information from the patient/patient's representative for patient profile (e.g., diagnosis or desired therapeutic outcome, allergies, adverse reactions, medical history)
2. Obtain information from prescriber and/or health care professionals for patient profile (e.g., diagnosis or desired therapeutic outcome, allergies, adverse reactions, medical history)
3. Assess prescription/medication order for completeness, correctness, authenticity, and legality
4. Assess prescription/medication order for appropriateness (e.g., drug selection, dosage, drug interactions, dosage form, delivery system)
5. Evaluate the medical record/patient profile for any or all of the following: disease states, clinical condition, medication use, allergies, adverse reactions, disabilities, medical/surgical therapies, laboratory findings, physical assessments and/or diagnostic tests
6. Perform physical assessment (e.g., vital signs/blood pressure measurement, observations of signs/symptoms)
7. Perform health screening (e.g., blood glucose checks, diagnostic tests)
8. Evaluate the pharmaceutical information needs of the patient/patient's representative

### B. Dispense Medications

1. Select specific product(s) to be dispensed for a prescription/medication order
2. Document preparation of medication in various dosage forms (e.g., compounded, repackaging)
3. Document preparation of controlled substances for dispensing
4. Verify label(s) for prescription containers
5. Select auxiliary label(s) for container(s)
6. Perform the final check for medications, products, preparations, or devices prior to dispensing
7. Use automated dispensing machines
8. Administer medications, biologicals, and immunizations as ordered by a prescriber, protocol, or scope of practice
9. Participate in compounding (sterile and non-sterile)

## California Board of Pharmacy Content Outline

**2. PATIENT OUTCOMES**        **33 items**

### A. Determine a Course of Action

1. Develop a therapeutic regimen for prescription medications (e.g., recommend alteration of prescribed drug regimen, select drug if necessary, perform medication therapy management)
2. Collaborate with health care team/prescriber to determine goals of therapy and course of action
3. Assess changes in health status (e.g., onset of new disease states, changes in clinical condition)
4. Perform pharmacokinetic calculations
5. Perform monitoring and therapeutic management activities
6. Manage drug therapy according to protocols or scope of practice
7. Resolve problems that arise with patient's therapy (e.g., ADEs, drug interactions, non-adherence)
8. Apply results of literature in the performance of evidence-based pharmacotherapy
9. Assess patient for immunization needs
10. Resolve problems with insurance coverage of prescription, medication, or device orders
11. Perform medication reconciliation
12. Recommend/order necessary monitoring procedures (e.g., renal/hepatic function, glucose levels, EKG, drug levels)
13. Initiate pharmacist-provider therapies (e.g., hormonal contraceptives, smoking cessation, travel-related medications)

### B. Educate Patients and Health Care Professionals

1. Assess the patient's understanding of the disease and treatment
2. Counsel patient/patient's representative regarding prescription medication therapy and devices
3. Counsel patient/patient's representative regarding nonprescription medication (OTC)
4. Counsel patient/patient's representative regarding herbal/complementary/alternative therapies
5. Counsel patient/patient's representative regarding non-drug therapy
6. Counsel patient/patient's representative regarding self-monitoring of therapy (e.g., devices, symptoms)
7. Verify the patient's/patient representative's understanding of the information presented
8. Educate health care professionals (e.g., physicians, nurses, medical residents/fellows, other health care providers/students, precepting intern pharmacists)
9. Communicate results of monitoring to patient/patient's representative, prescriber and/or other health care professionals
10. Respond to consumer inquiries (e.g. internet searches, media information, FDA patient safety alerts, radio/television commercials)
11. Provide supplemental information, as indicated (e.g., medication guides, computer-generated information)
12. Participate in emergency preparedness and response

### C. Promote Public Health

1. Participate in population health screening and/or disease or condition management programs
2. Participate in health-related public awareness/patient education programs
3. Make recommendations regarding health care resources for patients (e.g., Medicare Part D, patient assistance programs)

## 3. PHARMACY OPERATIONS                                          22 items

### A. Pharmaceuticals, Devices and Supplies, and Inventory Control

1. Ensure quality specifications for pharmaceuticals, durable medical equipment, devices, and supplies (e.g., sourcing, pedigree)
2. Place orders for pharmaceuticals, durable medical equipment, devices, and supplies, including expediting of emergency orders
3. Maintain a record-keeping system of items purchased/received/returned in compliance with legal requirements (e.g., dangerous drugs, devices, supplies)
4. Maintain a record of controlled substances ordered, received, stored, and removed from inventory
5. Dispose of expired, returned, or recalled pharmaceuticals, durable medical equipment, devices, supplies, and document actions taken
6. Respond to changes in product availability (e.g., drug shortages, recalls)
7. Design and implement policies to prevent theft and/or drug diversion
8. Comply with policies and procedures to prevent theft and/or drug diversion

### B. Perform Quality Assurance/Improvement

1. Assess pharmacist and/or pharmacy technician competence
2. Ensure the accuracy of medication administration
3. Participate in a system to monitor/improve medication use including quality assurance programs (e.g., antimicrobial stewardship, standard order sets, peer review, self-evaluation)
4. Participate in a system for medication error prevention, assessment, and reporting (e.g., root cause analysis, National Patient Safety Goals, medication error reduction program)
5. Participate in systems by which adverse drug effects and interactions are prevented, documented, evaluated, and reported

### C. Manage Operations, Human Resources and Information Systems

1. Monitor the practice site and/or service area for compliance with federal, state, and local laws, regulations, and professional standards/guidelines
2. Supervise the work of pharmacy personnel
3. Ensure the availability, control, and confidentiality of patient and prescription information (e.g., patient profiles, medication administration records)
4. Participate in the development of pharmacy policies and procedures, protocols, order sets, and/or therapeutic guidelines
5. Participate in the use of pharmacy information systems and technology (e.g., electronic health record, e-prescribing, CURES)
6. Manage the use of pharmacy information systems and technology (e.g., electronic health record, e-prescribing, CURES)

## California Board of Pharmacy Content Outline

**D. Manage Formulary and Medication Use Systems**
1. Use a formulary system (e.g., therapeutic conversion, advising patients and prescribers)

2. Manage an existing formulary system (e.g., formulary guidelines, criteria for use, tier placement, evaluation of products for inclusion)
3. Apply therapeutic interchanges
4. Design medication use evaluations (e.g., set criteria, establish data collection process)
5. Analyze medication use evaluation data
6. Apply results of medication use evaluations to revise practice procedures to improve patient outcomes

**Total 75 items**

Fifteen pretest items will be included on each test form.

# 2

# Regulation of Pharmacy Practice

This section reviews California law for dispensing prescriptions and primarily covers non-controlled substances. Regulations for controlled substances are more stringent and are reviewed separately.

## CALIFORNIA BOARD OF PHARMACY

Image courtesy of the California Board of Pharmacy

The board's vision statement is "Healthy Californians through quality pharmacist's care. "

The board protects and promotes the health and safety of Californians by pursuing the highest quality of pharmacist's care and the appropriate use of pharmaceuticals through education, communication, licensing, legislation, regulation, and enforcement.

The board includes 13 members, each of whom serves 1 or 2 four-year terms. The board elects a president, a vice president, and a treasurer. The board may appoint an executive officer, who may (or may not) be a board member.

The board oversees all aspects of pharmacy practice, including the pharmacists, the pharmacies, and the products (drugs and devices). Additionally, the board regulates drug wholesalers and other facilities that store and furnish prescription drugs. Pharmacy inspectors work for the board and ensure legal compliance with the pharmacy laws. They have the power to arrest, without a warrant, a person who they believe has violated the pharmacy laws.

## DUTIES AND LICENSURE OF THE PHARMACY STAFF

Pharmacists, interns, pharmacy technicians, and pharmacy technician trainees must wear name tags when at work, in 18-point type, that contain their name and license status.[8] All licensees must also join the board's email notification list.[9]

8   B&PC 680, B&PC 4115.5(e), CCR 1793.7(c)
9   B&PC 4013(d)

## Pharmacist-in-Charge

Each pharmacy must have a pharmacist-in-charge (PIC) who is responsible for the daily operations of the pharmacy. The PIC has adequate authority to make sure that the pharmacy is compliant with both federal and state law. The PIC has strict liability for violation of the law in the pharmacy, even if he or she did not have actual knowledge of the violation. The PIC can supervise up to 2 pharmacies as long as they are within 50 driving miles of each other.[10] Any change of PIC is reported by the pharmacy and the departing PIC to the board in writing within 30 days. It is not permissible for a pharmacist to be a PIC of a pharmacy and a designated representative-in-charge (DRIC) for a wholesaler or a veterinary food-animal drug retailer at the same time.

The PIC must complete a biennial (every other year) self-assessment form for their pharmacy before July 1 of each odd numbered year (by July 1, 2017, then again by July 1, 2019). An additional self-assessment form must be completed within 30 days if a new permit is issued, when the pharmacy has a new PIC, and when the pharmacy moves to a new location. Each self-assessment form will be kept in the pharmacy for 3 years. The self-assessment form is not sent to anyone, but if the pharmacy is visited by an inspector they will need to produce the form and the inspector will compare the actual situation in the pharmacy to what is on the form.

## Pharmacist

The traditional role of a pharmacist is the safe and proper dispensing of medications. The pharmacist receives new prescriptions, interprets the prescriptions, interprets the clinical data in the patient's medication records, consults with other healthcare professionals, performs drug utilization reviews (DURs), provides counseling, and supervises the pharmacy staff.

It is common in smaller pharmacies for there to be only one pharmacist on duty, and if the pharmacist leaves for a break, there will be no pharmacist present. In such a case, the pharmacist can leave the pharmacy for breaks and meal periods for up to 30 minutes. The pharmacy can stay open and the pharmacist does not need to stay in the pharmacy area during the break. The ancillary staff (intern pharmacists, pharmacy technicians, clerks) can stay in the pharmacy if the pharmacist believes that the drugs and devices will be secure when he or she is gone. During this time, the staff can continue to perform non-discretionary duties. Interns cannot counsel patients when there is no pharmacist to supervise. Any duty performed by other staff members must be reviewed by the pharmacist upon his or her return to the pharmacy. While the pharmacist is away, only refill medications that the pharmacist has already checked and which do not require patient counseling can be dispensed. New medications (initial fills) cannot be dispensed while the pharmacist is gone because these would require an offer to counsel.[11]

10   CCR 1709.1
11   B&PC 1714.1

The passing of Senate Bill 493 has expanded the scope of practice for all registered pharmacists and created a new type of license called the advanced practice pharmacist.

Under SB 493, all registered pharmacists (RPhs) can provide the following services after meeting certain training requirements:[12]

- Administer drugs and biologics when ordered by a prescriber. Previously, pharmacists were permitted to administer only oral and topical drugs. Pharmacists can now administer drugs by other routes, including by injection.

- Provide consultation, training and education about drug therapy, disease management and disease prevention.

- Participate in multidisciplinary reviews of patient progress, which includes appropriate access to medical records.

- Furnish self-administered hormonal contraceptives, which includes oral formulations (birth control pills), transdermal (the patch, such as *Xulane*), vaginal (the ring, such as *NuvaRing*) and by injection (such as *Depo-SubQ Provera*).

- Furnish travel medications recommended by the CDC and which do not require a diagnosis.

- Furnish prescription nicotine replacement products for smoking cessation, including the inhaler (such as *Nicotrol*) and the nasal spray (such as *Nicotrol NS*).

- Independently initiate and administer immunizations published by the CDC to patients 3 years and older. A physician protocol is still required to administer immunizations on children younger than 3 years.

- Order and interpret tests for the purpose of monitoring and managing the efficacy and toxicity of drug therapies, in coordination with the patient's primary care provider (PCP) or with the diagnosing prescriber.

To be licensed as a pharmacist, a candidate must meet the following requirements:[13]

- Be at least 18 years old.

- Must have graduated from an ACPE-accredited school of pharmacy or be a graduate of a foreign school of pharmacy and be certified by NABP's Foreign Pharmacy Graduate Examination Committee (FPGEC).

- Have completed at least 150 hours of semester college credit, 90 of which must be from a pharmacy school. Have received at least a baccalaureate degree in a course of study devoted to pharmacy.

12  B&PC 4052
13  B&PC 4200

- Must have completed <u>1,500 hours of pharmacy practice experience,</u> and 900 of the hours must be completed in a pharmacy, with experience in both community and institutional settings. The intern hours affidavits must be signed by the pharmacist under whom the experience was earned. Intern pharmacists that graduated after January 1, 2016 from an <u>ACPE-accredited school of pharmacy</u> must be deemed to have satisfied the pharmacy practice experience hours.[14]

- Must have passed the NAPLEX and CPJE. A person who has failed the CPJE 4 times will need to enroll in an ACPE-accredited school of pharmacy in order to complete 16 semester units of additional coursework in pharmacy before they are able to retake the exam.

- Must have passed a criminal background check.

- If a licensee in another state moves to California because their partner is stationed here with a division of the US Armed Forces, the board will expedite the licensure process.

In order to ensure that pharmacists are up-to-date with new drug changes and treatment guidelines, <u>30 hours</u> of continuing education (CE) must be completed during each 2-year license period.[15] For license renewals on or after July 1, 2019, at least <u>2 hours of pharmacy law and ethics</u> must be included for each renewal. The license expires on the <u>last day of the pharmacist's birth month</u>. The first 2-year license cycle is <u>exempt</u> from CE requirements since the pharmacist is considered up-to-date. The certificate of completion of CEs must be kept for <u>4 years</u>.

Pharmacists must disclose (on the renewal form) if any government agency issued any <u>disciplinary action</u> against <u>any of their licenses</u> that resulted in a <u>restriction</u> or <u>penalty</u> being placed on the license, such as revocation, suspension, probation, public reprimand, or reproval. Pharmacists must disclose on the license renewal form if they have been <u>convicted of any violation of law</u>, except for traffic violations that do not involve <u>alcohol</u> or <u>controlled substances</u>. Electronic fingerprints must be on file with the board.[16]

---

14  B&PC 4209
15  CCR 1732.5
16  CCR 1702

## Advanced Practice Pharmacist

The advanced practice pharmacist (APh) license enables pharmacists to provide clinical services in various settings. The role of an APh is similar to that of clinical pharmacists in a hospital or ambulatory care setting. Historically, and in the absence of provider status, clinical services have been performed under a collaborative practice agreement (CPA) or protocol. APhs can do the following:[17]

■ Perform patient assessments.

■ Order and interpret drug therapy-related tests in coordination with the patient's PCP or with the diagnosing prescriber.

■ Refer patients to other healthcare providers.

■ Participate in the evaluation and management of diseases and health conditions in collaboration with other healthcare providers.

■ Initiate, adjust, and discontinue drug therapy pursuant to an order by a patient's treating prescriber and in accordance with established protocols. If the APh is initiating or adjusting a controlled substance therapy, the APh must be registered with the Drug Enforcement Administration.

In order to be recognized as an APh, a pharmacist must meet two of the three following requirements:[18]

■ Earn certification in a relevant area of practice, such as ambulatory care, critical care, oncology pharmacy or pharmacotherapy.[19,20,21]

■ Complete a postgraduate residency program.

Have provided clinical services to patients for one year (and at least 1,500 hours) under a CPA or protocol with a physician, an advanced practice pharmacist, a pharmacist practicing collaborative drug therapy management (CDTM), or within a health system.[22]

17   B&PC 4052.6
18   B&PC 4210
19   CCR 1730.2
20   http://appharmacist.com/ (accessed 2018 Feb 16).
21   http://www.cshp.org/page/Certificate_Programs (accessed 2018 Feb 16).
22   CCR 1730.1(a)(3)

## Intern Pharmacist

An intern pharmacist can perform almost all functions of a pharmacist at the discretion of and under the supervision of a pharmacist. The intern pharmacists <u>cannot have a key</u> to the pharmacy. All prescriptions filled by an intern pharmacist are checked by a pharmacist before dispensing.[23]

A pharmacist can supervise <u>2 interns at any one time</u>. During a temporary absence of a pharmacist, including during breaks, an intern pharmacist may not perform any discretionary duties nor act as a pharmacist. This means that the intern pharmacist can only perform the duties of a technician when there is no pharmacist present.

In order to be registered as an intern pharmacist, the candidate must meet one of the following requirements:[24]

- Be currently enrolled as a student in a pharmacy school that is ACPE-accredited or which is recognized by the board.

- Be a graduate of a school of pharmacy that is ACPE-accredited or which is recognized by the board and who also has an application pending to become licensed as a pharmacist in California.

- Be a graduate of a foreign pharmacy school who has obtained certification from NABP's Foreign Pharmacy Graduate Examination Committee (FPGEC). This is obtained after passing an English competency test (TOEFL) and the Foreign Pharmacy Graduate Equivalency Examination (FPGEE).

## Pharmacy Technician

Pharmacy technicians assist the pharmacists with dispensing prescription drugs. In California, technicians are permitted to perform packaging, manipulative, repetitive, or other <u>nondiscretionary tasks</u> under the direct supervision of a pharmacist.[25] "Non-discretionary" means that the work does not include the ability to make decisions according to the technician's judgment; this is left to the pharmacist. Non-discretionary tasks, rather, are routine and repetitive, and include removing drugs from stock,  counting, pouring or mixing pharmaceuticals, placing the product into containers and applying the label to a prescription bottle.

Outpatient prescriptions filled by a pharmacy technician must be checked by a pharmacist. In the hospital setting, technicians can check the work of other technician. Each pharmacy will need to have job descriptions for the pharmacy technicians that work at that location, and written policies and procedures to ensure compliance with California's legal requirements.

23   CCR 1717(b)(1)
24   B&PC 4208
25   B&PC 4115

### Technician Checking Technician Programs

Pharmacy technicians who have received specialized training can participate in a technician checking technician (TCT) program in <u>hospital</u> settings. After a technician has finished filling or replenishing the <u>unit dose distribution system, floor stock, or ward stock,</u> another technician (instead of a pharmacist) can check the accuracy of the work. The TCT program is permitted only in acute care hospitals that have an ongoing <u>clinical pharmacy program</u>, and which has <u>pharmacists located in the patient care areas.</u> "Prescriptions" in acute care facilities are called medication orders, and the medication orders must have been verified by the pharmacist. The technicians involved with TCT cannot approve the orders; they can only confirm the accuracy of the filling.

A pharmacist must check <u>compounded</u> and <u>repackaged</u> drugs before a technician uses it to fill unit dose distribution systems and floor/ward stock. The pharmacy must have on file a description of the hospital's clinical program before starting a TCT program. The PIC will need to carefully monitor the program to ensure that the requirements outlined in the hospital's TCT P&P are in place. A pharmacy technician assigned to this activity must have received specialized training, which will be outlined in the TCT P&P.

### Ratio of Technicians to Pharmacists

In the community setting, <u>1 technician is permitted for the first pharmacist</u> on duty, and <u>2 technicians are permitted for each additional pharmacist</u>. If there is 1 pharmacist on duty, there can only be 1 technician. If there are 2 pharmacists on duty, there can be 3 technicians, if there are 3 pharmacists, there can be 5 technicians, and so forth.[26]

The ratio of technicians to pharmacists in the institutional (i.e., hospital) setting is 2 technicians for each pharmacist on duty.[27]

### Technician Licensure

An individual can become licensed as a pharmacy technician if he or she is a high school graduate or possesses a general educational development (GED) certificate equivalent, and meets any one of the following requirements:[28]

■ Obtained an associate's degree in pharmacy technology.

■ Completed a course of training specified by the board.

■ Graduated from a school of pharmacy recognized by the board.

---

26   B&PC 4115(f)(1)
27   B&PC 4115(f)(2), CCR 1793.7(f)
28   B&PC 4202

■ Completed a board-approved certification program accredited by the National Commission for Certifying Agencies. This includes both the Pharmacy Technician Certification Board (PTCB) and the National Healthcareer Association (NHA) programs.

## Pharmacy Technician Trainee

A pharmacy technician trainee is a person who is required to complete an externship as part of their educational program to become a pharmacy technician. The purpose of the externship is to gain practical training experience. The trainee will be able to perform packaging, manipulative, repetitive, or other nondiscretionary tasks, which must be under the direct supervision of a pharmacist.[29]

A pharmacist can only supervise 1 technician trainee at a time, and only for up to 120 hours.

## Pharmacy Clerk

A non-licensed person (clerk/typist) can type a prescription label and enter prescription information into a computer, and request and receive refill authorizations.[30] A clerk is not allowed to pull drugs from the shelf or fill prescription medications. However, clerks can put drugs on the shelf and give patients their prescriptions at the point of transaction. There are no maximum limits on the number of clerks allowed to be in the pharmacy at one time. There can be as many clerks as the pharmacist feels that he or she can reasonably supervise.

## REQUIREMENTS FOR VALID PRESCRIPTIONS

### Healthcare Providers Authorized to Prescribe Medications

Some healthcare providers can prescribe independently while other healthcare providers can only dependently prescribe under a physician-directed protocol.[31] Any prescriber that prescribes for controlled substances must be registered with the DEA. Pharmacists should not fill a prescription if the practitioner is not prescribing within his or her scope of practice.

An employee or agent (such as a nurse or secretary), under the supervision of a prescriber, can transmit prescriptions for non controlled and schedule III – V drugs to a pharmacist.[32] The pharmacist must document who is calling in or faxing the prescription on behalf of the prescriber.[33] The agent can also prepare the prescription for the prescriber to sign and date.

29  B&PC 4115.5
30  CCR 1793.3
31  H&SC 11150
32  https://www.deadiversion.usdoj.gov/fed_regs/rules/2010/fr1006.htm (accessed 2018 Feb 16).
33  B&PC 4071

| HEALTHCARE PROVIDER | TYPE OF PRESCRIBING/FURNISHING AUTHORITY |
| --- | --- |
| Physician (MD/DO) | Independent authority<br><br>■ Non-controlled and schedule II – V drugs; if prescribing scheduled drugs will need to register with the DEA and get a DEA number. |
| Dentist | Independent authority, limited to scope of practice<br><br>■ Non-controlled and schedule II – V drugs; if prescribing scheduled drugs will need to register with the DEA and get a DEA number. |
| Podiatrist (DPM) | Independent authority, limited to scope of practice<br><br>■ Non-controlled and schedule II – V drugs; if prescribing scheduled drugs will need to register with the DEA and get a DEA number. |
| Veterinarian (DVM) | Independent authority, limited to scope of practice<br><br>■ Non-controlled and schedule II – V drugs; if prescribing scheduled drugs will need to register with the DEA and get a DEA number. |
| Optometrist (OD) | Independent authority, limited to scope of practice<br><br>Must be certified with the Board of Optometry to prescribe drugs. These optometrists will have a letter T at the end of their license number.[34]<br><br>For codeine-containing or hydrocodone-containing products, can prescribe a max 3-day supply. If prescribing scheduled drugs will need to register with the DEA and get a DEA number.[35]<br><br>Optometrists can prescribe other drugs relevant to their practice, including oral analgesics, OTC drugs, oral antibiotics, topical antibiotics/antivirals/anesthetics/lubricants/anti-inflammatories (including NSAIDs and steroid eye drops)/antihistamines, diagnostic drops (such as atropine and other mydriatics used to dilate the pupils) and glaucoma eye drops.[36] |
| Naturopathic Doctors (ND) | Independent authority, limited to the following:<br><br>■ Epinephrine to treat anaphylaxis<br>■ Natural and synthetic hormones (naturopathic doctor must have a DEA number to prescribe controlled substances, including testosterone[37, 38])<br>■ Vitamins, minerals, amino acids, glutathione, botanicals and their extracts, homeopathic medicines, electrolytes, sugars, and diluents, only when such substances are available without a prescription.<br><br>A furnishing number is required for NDs to prescribe. It is typically the ND's license number preceded by the letters NDF.<br><br>Dependent authority:<br><br>■ All other non-controlled and schedule III – V drugs; if prescribing scheduled drugs will need to register with the DEA and get a DEA number. |
| Registered Pharmacist (RPh) | Independent authority, limited to the following:<br><br>■ Emergency contraception, self-administered hormonal contraception<br>■ Travel medicine recommended by the CDC, not requiring a diagnosis<br>■ Routine immunizations published by the CDC for 3+ years old<br>■ Naloxone<br>■ Prescription nicotine replacement products<br><br>Dependent authority:<br><br>■ All other non-controlled and schedule II – V drugs; if prescribing scheduled drugs will need to register with the DEA and get a DEA number. |

34  B&PC 3041(b)
35  B&PC 3041(b)(14)
36  B&PC 3041(b)(13)
37  http://www.naturopathic.ca.gov/licensees/notice_hormone.shtml (accessed 2018 Feb 16).
38  http://www.pharmacy.ca.gov/publications/05_oct_script.pdf (accessed 2018 Feb 16).

| HEALTHCARE PROVIDER | TYPE OF PRESCRIBING/FURNISHING AUTHORITY |
|---|---|
| Certified Nurse-Midwife (CNM) | Dependent authority<br>■ Non-controlled and schedule II – V drugs; if prescribing scheduled drugs will need to register with the DEA and get a DEA number. |
| Nurse Practitioner (NP) | Dependent authority<br>■ Non-controlled and schedule II – V drugs; if prescribing scheduled drugs will need to register with the DEA and get a DEA number. |
| Physician Assistant (PA) | Dependent authority<br>■ Non-controlled and schedule II – V drugs; if prescribing scheduled drugs will need to register with the DEA and get a DEA number. |

## Self-Prescribing and Prescribing for Family Members

In California, prescribers can self-prescribe non-controlled substances.[39] Prescribers can prescribe non-controlled and controlled substances to family members as long as there is a valid physician/patient relationship, a legitimate medical purpose, and a good faith exam.[40] Pharmacists should be wary of drug diversion before dispensing.

## Prescriptions from Deceased Prescribers

If a valid prescription was written when the prescriber was living, the prescription is considered valid until all refills are gone, and no more than 6 months from the date written for controlled substances[41] and one year for non-controlled substances (standard of practice).[42]

However, the pharmacist should encourage the patient to look for a new doctor as soon as possible and not to wait until the prescription is expired or the refills are gone. If another doctor takes over the deceased prescriber's practice, the pharmacist should request a new prescription for refills because the patient now has a new prescriber.

## Prescriptions from Other States or Territories

A pharmacist can furnish a drug or device pursuant to a written or oral order from a prescriber licensed in a state other than California if the out-of-state prescriber has a license equivalent to that required of a California prescriber.[43,44] The pharmacist may need to verify the prescriber's license and determine whether he or she is authorized to prescribe. The pharmacist can then dispense the prescription directly to the patient.

See the Controlled Substances section for further discussion, such as the requirement for security forms.

39  H&SC 11170
40  http://www.pharmacy.ca.gov/publications/13_mar_script.pdf (accessed 2018 Feb 16).
41  H&SC 11166
42  http://www.pharmacy.ca.gov/publications/13_fall_script.pdf (accessed 2018 Feb 16).
43  http://www.pharmacy.ca.gov/publications/07_jul_script.pdf (accessed 2018 Feb 16).
44  CCR 1717(d)

## Prescriptions from Foreign Countries

As a general rule, a pharmacist cannot fill a prescription from another country. The District of Columbia and the U.S. territories (which include Puerto Rico, the Virgin Islands, Guam, and American Samoa) are treated the same as U.S. states for filling prescriptions.

## Written, Oral, Electronic, and Faxed Prescriptions

A prescription must have the following information:[45]

- The name of the patient

- The address of the patient

- The name and quantity of the drug or device prescribed

- The directions for use

- The date of issue

- Prescriber information (rubber stamped, typed, or printed by hand or typeset):
  - The name, address, and telephone number
  - Prescriber's license classification
  - Prescriber's DEA number, if a controlled substance is prescribed
- Condition or purpose of prescribed drug, if requested by the patient

- Prescriber's signature

If the prescription is written by a veterinarian for a controlled substance for an animal it must state the <u>kind of animal</u> and the <u>name and address of the owner</u> or person having custody of the animal.[46]

Orally transmitted prescriptions are received and reduced to writing only by a pharmacist or intern pharmacist working under the direct supervision of a pharmacist.[47] To "reduce to writing" means to write the oral prescription onto the pharmacy's prescription blank. If orally transmitted, the pharmacist who received the prescription is identified by initialing the prescription, and if dispensed by another pharmacist, the dispensing pharmacist also initials the prescription.

Faxed prescriptions are received only from a prescriber's office (not from the patient) and reduced to hard copy.

Internet prescriptions for patients should only be dispensed if the prescriber has performed an examination.

45  B&PC 4040
46  H&SC 11241
47  B&PC 4070

The name or initials of the dispensing pharmacist must be documented for each prescription. Commonly, the pharmacist will <u>handwrite</u> their initials on the pharmacy's duplicate copy of prescription label or use a unique login for an electronic pharmacy workflow software which will <u>electronically document</u> who verified each prescription. [48, 49]

The prescription must be kept for <u>3 years</u>.

## Written Prescriptions for Medi-Cal Outpatient Drugs

Since April 1, 2008, the federal Centers for Medicare and Medicaid Services (CMS) has required that all <u>written, non-electronic prescriptions</u> must be on <u>tamper-resistant</u> pads for all <u>Medi-Cal outpatient drugs</u> (including over-the-counter drugs, non-controlled drugs, and controlled substances) in order to be <u>reimbursable</u> by the federal government. The tamper-resistant pad must meet three requirements:[50]

| SECURITY FEATURES | EXAMPLES |
|---|---|
| Prevent unauthorized copying of a completed or blank prescription form. | ■ The word "void" appears when this prescription is photocopied<br>■ Forms with watermarks |
| Prevent the erasure or modification of information written on the prescription by the provider. | ■ Quantity check off boxes so that the prescriber can indicate the quantity by checking the applicable box<br>■ Check boxes must be printed on the form so that the prescriber can indicate the number of refills ordered.<br>■ Preprinted text "Rx is void if more than ___ Rxs on paper" on prescription paper:" |
| Prevent the use of counterfeit prescription. | ■ Each prescription form is serially numbered<br>■ Certain text or images are printed in thermochromic ink |

The California Board of Pharmacy requires certain security features on prescription forms used to prescribe controlled substances.[51] A <u>California security form</u> for controlled substances <u>exceeds the Medi-Cal prescription requirements</u> for outpatient drugs.[52] Therefore, a California security form can also be used to prescribe outpatient drugs for Medi-Cal beneficiaries. California security forms are discussed further in the Controlled Substances section.

## Correcting Errors or Omissions on Prescriptions

Errors or omissions on a prescription for non-controlled drugs can be revised by the pharmacist if it is minor (such as misspelling a drug name) or after consultation with the prescriber if it is significant. The pharmacist will need to document the discussion. Alternatively, after verification with the prescriber, the prescription can be re-written as an oral prescription and the original prescription will be voided. Or, the prescriber will resend another prescription via electronic transmission or fax.[53]

48   CCR 1717(b)(1)
49   CCR 1712(a)
50   https://files.medi-cal.ca.gov/pubsdoco/newsroom/newsroom_8840.asp (accessed 2018 Feb 16).
51   H&SC 11164(a)
52   http://www.pharmacy.ca.gov/publications/17_jun_script.pdf (accessed 2018 Feb 16).
53   CCR 1761

See the Controlled Substances section on how to correct errors or omissions on controlled substance prescriptions; these have more rigid requirements due to the risk of diversion.

## PRESCRIPTION DROP BOX

A patient or the patient's agent can deposit a prescription into a secure container (a drop box) that is at the same address as the pharmacy. If a pharmacy chooses to use a drop box, the pharmacy is responsible for the security and confidentiality of the prescriptions placed into the drop box.[54]

## PRESCRIPTION REFILLS

Refill authorization from the prescriber is obtained before refilling a prescription.[55]

It is standard of practice to stop dispensing prescriptions for non-scheduled drugs after one year from the issue date. Although there is no refill limit for non-scheduled drugs, it should not be dispensed after one year from date of issue.

All scheduled drugs expire 6 months from the date of issue. There are no refill limits for schedule V drugs, but there are restrictions for schedule III and IV drugs. Refills for schedule III and IV drug prescriptions are limited to a maximum of 5 refills within 6 months, and all refills combined cannot exceed a 120-day supply. The original fill is not a refill, and is not included when determining if the 120-day supply limit has been exceeded.

Refills for Schedule II controlled substances are prohibited. See the Controlled Substances section for further discussion.

### PRN Refills

PRN (as-needed) refills are acceptable for non-controlled substances, according to California law. Since it is standard of practice that prescriptions for non-controlled substances expire 1 year from date of issue, PRN refills should not be refilled past one year from the date of issue.

If a prescription has PRN refills, expires within a year, and is written for a 30-day supply per fill, then it can be refilled 11 times before it expires. The pharmacist can dispense the original fill and 11 more refills. Notice that the amount of refills allowed depends on the day supply the prescription is written for. If it is written for a 90-day supply, then the pharmacist can dispense the original fill and 3 refills before the prescription expires.

PRN refills for controlled substances are not acceptable.[56]

---

54   CCR 1713 (c)
55   B&PC 4063
56   B&PC 4063

## Emergency Refills Without the Prescriber's Authorization

Prescriptions for non-controlled drugs and schedule III – V drugs can be filled without the prescriber's authorization if the prescriber is unavailable to authorize the refill and if, in the pharmacist's professional judgment, failure to refill the prescription might interrupt the patient's ongoing care and have a <u>significant adverse effect</u> on the patient's well-being.[57] The pharmacist must make every reasonable effort to contact the prescriber. The emergency refill must be properly documented and the prescriber must be notified of the emergency refill within a reasonable amount of time.

California <u>does not specify a quantity limit</u> for an emergency refill for <u>non-controlled drugs</u>, and the pharmacist will use his or her professional judgment when deciding to give a full or partial refill amount.[58] For <u>schedule III – V drugs</u>, the pharmacist can only provide a <u>reasonable amount</u> to cover the emergency period until the prescriber can be contacted for a refill authorization. For controlled substances, the pharmacist must note on the reverse side of the prescription the date and quantity of the refill and that the prescriber was not available and the <u>reason</u> to refill the prescription without the prescriber's authorization.[59]

Pharmacists cannot dispense an emergency refill for <u>schedule II drugs</u> since these prescriptions <u>cannot have refills</u>. At the very least, an <u>emergency verbal order</u> must be obtained for schedule II drugs. This is discussed further in the Controlled Substances section.

## CONVERTING A 30-DAY PRESCRIPTION TO A 90-DAY PRESCRIPTION

A patient may prefer to convert a prescription from a 30-day supply to a 90-day supply to minimize trips to the pharmacy or to save on prescription copays. It is permissible to dispense <u>up to a 90-day supply</u> of a <u>non-controlled, non-psychiatric</u> drug when the initial prescription specified a shorter time period (e.g., a 30-day supply) as long as the following requirements are met:[60]

- The patient has completed an <u>initial 30-day supply</u> of the drug with no negative effects, or the patient previously received the same medication with a 90-day supply.

- The <u>total quantity dispensed</u> (including the refills) <u>does not exceed the amount authorized</u> on the prescription.

- The pharmacist notifies the prescriber of the increase in the number of days supply dispensed.

A pharmacist cannot dispense a greater supply of a drug if:

- The prescriber indicates, either orally or in his or her own handwriting, "No change to quantity," or words of similar meaning.

- The prescriber indicates that dispensing the initial amount (such as a 30-day supply) is medically necessary.

57  B&PC 4064, H&SC 11201
58  B&PC 4064(a)
59  H&SC 11201
60  B&PC 4064.5 (a-e)

## DISPENSING A 12-MONTH SUPPLY OF HORMONAL CONTRACEPTIVES AT ONCE

California has expanded patient access to self-administered hormonal contraceptives (birth control) by allowing patients to pick up an annual supply all at once. Self-administered hormonal contraceptives include the pill, the patch, (e.g., *Xulane*), the ring (e.g., *NuvaRing*) and the injection (e.g., *Depo-SubQ Provera*). Health plans are required to provide coverage for up to a 12-month supply.[61] Dispensing an annual supply has many benefits, including increased adherence, which reduces unintended pregnancies. This decreases healthcare costs by reducing the number of pregnancy tests and pregnancies.[62]

At a patient's request and with a valid prescription, the pharmacy must dispense up to a 12-month supply of a self-administered hormonal contraceptive (all at one time).[63] If a patient presents a prescription for *Sprintec* #28 tablets and 11 refills, the patient can request for the entire annual supply to be dispensed at once. The total quantity dispensed (including the refills) cannot exceed the amount authorized on the prescription. If the prescriber only authorized a prescription for *Sprintec* #28 tablets and 2 refills, then the pharmacist can only dispense a 3-month supply all at once. If the prescriber indicates that there cannot be any change to the quantity or if the prescriber indicates that dispensing the initial amount is medically necessary, the pharmacist must dispense the quantity the prescriber has specified.

A pharmacist can also furnish an annual supply of self-administered hormonal contraceptive to a patient. The discussion on Furnishing Self-Administered Hormonal Contraceptives in this manual explains how a pharmacist can furnish contraception without a prescription under the board-provided protocol.[64]

Pharmacists have the right to refuse dispensing or furnishing hormonal contraceptives if it is against their ethical, moral, or religious beliefs. Keep in mind that while the pharmacist has the right to work according to their personal beliefs, the employer has a right not to hire them. The employer may feel that the patients who frequent that pharmacy could have medical needs (i.e., contraception) that will not be met. See the discussion on Refusal to Dispense Based on Religious, Moral or Ethical Beliefs in this manual.

61   H&SC 1367.25(d)
62   SB-999
63   B&PC 4064.5(f)
64   B&PC 4052.3

## PRESCRIPTION TRANSFERS

Prescriptions can be transferred from one pharmacy to another. This must be done by direct communication between two <u>pharmacists</u> or <u>interns</u>.[65] Prescriptions for <u>non-controlled drugs</u> can be transferred <u>as many times as there are refills remaining</u>.

Information kept by each pharmacy must at least include:

- Identification of the pharmacists or intern pharmacists involved in transferring information between the two pharmacies.

- Name and identification code (i.e., pharmacy store number) or address of the pharmacy from which the prescription was received or to which the prescription was transferred. Each pharmacy receives the other pharmacy's information.

- Original date and last dispensing date.

- Number of refills and date originally authorized.

- Number of refills transferred (remaining refills that have not dispensed).

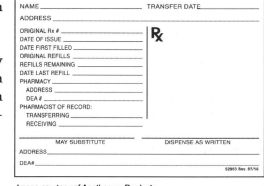

Image courtesy of Apothecary Products

See the Controlled Substances section for further discussion on transferring prescriptions for controlled substances. Schedule II drugs do not have refills; thus, no transfer of refills is possible.

## LABELING REQUIREMENTS FOR PRESCRIPTION CONTAINERS

Prescription containers must have all of the following information:[66]

- Drug name

- Directions for use

- Name of the patient or patients

- Name of the prescriber

- Date of issue (date the prescription was written)

- Name and address of the pharmacy

JOHNSON, JUDITH
VERAPAMIL ER 240 MG tablet
GENERIC FOR ISOPTIN SR
Manufacturer: Ivax Pharmaceutical
Take one tablet by mouth twice daily
Treats high blood pressure

Rx# 06197 1234567
DATE FILLED: 08/31/2018
ORIG RX DATE: 12/24/2018
RPH: #PT
Store DEA# BTS555555

Judith Johnson
5873 EVERGREEN AVE
DAVIS, CA 95616
(555) 555-7089

CAUTION: Federal law PROHIBITS the transfer of this drug to any person other than the patient for whom it was prescribed.

Prescriber: Roger Brown MD    Quantity: 60
Oblong ivory tablet 73  00 logo
Refills remaining: 3    Expires: 05/30/2018

Victor's Pharmacy
1625 N. Market Blvd.
Sacramento, CA 95834
(555) 555-9810

Image courtesy of the California Board of Pharmacy

65   CCR 1717(e)
66   B&PC 4076

- Prescription number

- Strength of drug

- Quantity of drug

- Expiration date

- Condition or purpose of the drug (if it is written on the prescription)

- Physical description of the drug (including the color, shape, and imprint; see container label example).

When a <u>brand name</u> drug is dispensed, the brand name should be listed on the prescription label (e.g., *Opana*). The manufacturer's name is not required because the brand name can be used to identify the manufacturer. *Opana* is a brand name drug manufactured by *Endo Pharmaceuticals*.

When a <u>generic</u> drug is dispensed, the label must include the <u>generic name</u>, the statement "<u>generic for</u> [insert brand name equivalent]" to indicate the <u>brand name drug equivalent</u> to the dispensed generic drug, and the <u>generic drug manufacturer</u> (e.g., Oxymorphone, generic for *Opana*, MFR: *Actavis*). There are often multiple manufacturers of the same generic drug (e.g., generic oxymorphone is manufactured by *Actavis, Teva, West-Ward, Sun* and ~10 other companies).

The expiration date written on the prescription label can be either the <u>expiration date on the manufacturer's container</u>, or <u>one year from the date the drug is dispensed</u>.[67] The expiration date will usually be notated with a month and year, with the drug acceptable to use until the end of the month in which it expires. For example, if the expiration date is 3/2018, then the expiration date is March 31, 2018. The monographs for some preparations state how the labeled expiration date must be determined. For example, the beyond-use date for reconstituted *Augmentin* is ten days. If a drug container <u>does not have an expiration date</u>, it is considered <u>misbranded</u>, is treated as an expired drug, and should not be dispensed.

See the Controlled Substances section for additional requirements on the labeling for scheduled drugs.

---

67   *http://www.pharmacy.ca.gov/publications/02_jan_script.pdf (accessed 2018 Feb 16).*

## Format

There are also formatting standards for multiple unit prescription labels. The goal of standardizing the labels is to promote patient understanding of the medication use, increase adherence, and reduce medication errors. The content of the prescription label is often the only drug information the patient will read. Thus, it has to be easy to understand and must include the proper auxiliary labels. These standards do not apply to inpatient medications since those are labeled for a healthcare professional to administer.

Each of the following items (and only these 4 items) must be clustered into one area of the label that comprises at least <u>50% of the label</u>. Each item must be printed in at least a <u>12-point sans serif typeface</u>, and listed in the following order:[68]

■ <u>Name of the patient</u>

■ <u>Name of the drug</u> (trade name alone or generic + "generic for _____" statement + the manufacturer) and <u>strength</u> of the drug.

■ The <u>directions for use</u> of the drug.

■ The <u>condition or purpose</u> for which the drug was prescribed if this was on the prescription.

For added emphasis, the label must also <u>highlight</u> in <u>bold</u> typeface or <u>color</u>, or use <u>blank space</u> to set off the 4 critical items above. All other, less critical information should not distract from the more important information listed above. Less critical information should be placed away from the items above (e.g., at the bottom of the label or in another less prominent location) to avoid distracting from the key information. These additional elements may appear in any style, font, and size typeface.

Directions for use should be clear and easy to interpret. Time periods should be specified and numbers should be used instead of alphabets when appropriate. For example, instead of "Take two tablets twice daily" the label should read "Take 2 tablets in the morning and 2 tablets in the evening". Avoid hourly intervals (such as "every 8 hours") since this requires the patient to count. In general, specifying an exact time should be avoided unless the drug must be taken at exact times (e.g., tacrolimus for a transplant patient, with times specified on the prescription, 12 hours apart). Specifying an exact time can be too restrictive for patients who are busy with work, school, or other responsibilities. Jargon or Latin terminology should not be used.

*68 CCR 1707.5*

## Translation

At the request of a patient or patient's representative, the pharmacist must provide translated directions for use, which must be printed on the prescription container, label, or on a supplemental document. If translated directions for use appear on a prescription container or label, the English language version of the directions also need to appear on the container or label, whenever possible, and can appear on other areas of the label outside of the patient centered area. When it is not possible for the English language directions for use to appear on the container or label, it should be provided on a supplemental document. A pharmacist can use translations made available by the board. A pharmacist is not required to provide translated directions for use beyond the languages that the board has made available in translated form.[69,70]

## Auxiliary Labels

Auxiliary labels are placed on the container and alert the patient to key warnings (such as "Do Not Drive a Car or Operate Heavy Machinery While Using This Medicine"), dietary requirements (such as "Take With Food") and storage requirements (such as "Keep in the Refrigerator). Auxiliary labels should be evidence-based and written in simple language. They should be placed in a standard place on the label and should be provided for each prescription in which the use is appropriate, rather than at the discretion of the pharmacist. See the Appendix for a list of common auxiliary labels.

According to the National Highway Transportation Safety Administration, 20% of drivers tested positive for drugs in 2014.[71] Drugs with central nervous system (CNS) depressant effects are particularly dangerous because they can slow down reaction time and subsequently cause motor vehicle accidents. To increase public awareness on the side effects of certain drugs and to reduce driving under the influence, the board has mandated warning labels for select drugs. Because the following classes of drugs may impair a person's ability to operate a vehicle or vessel, a pharmacist must include a warning on the prescription label of the drug container:[72]

- Muscle relaxants

- Antipsychotic drugs with CNS depressant effects

- Antidepressants with CNS depressant effects

- Antihistamines, motion sickness agents, antipruritics, antinauseants, anticonvulsants and antihypertensive agents with CNS depressant effects

- All controlled substances with CNS depressant effects

- Anticholinergic agents that may impair vision

69   http://www.pharmacy.ca.gov/publications/translations.shtml (accessed 2018 Feb 16).
70   B&PC 4076.6
71   https://www.nhtsa.gov/sites/nhtsa.dot.gov/files/812118-roadside_survey_2014.pdf (accessed 2018 Feb 16).
72   CCR 1744(a)

- Any other drug which, based on the pharmacist's professional judgment, may impair a patient's ability to operate a vehicle or vessel

Because the following classes of drugs pose a substantial risk to the person consuming the drug when taken <u>in combination with alcohol</u>, a pharmacist must include a warning on the prescription label:[73]

- <u>Disulfiram</u> and other drugs (e.g. , chlorpropamide, metronidazole) which may cause a <u>disulfiram-like reaction</u>

- <u>Monoamine oxidase inhibitors</u>

- <u>Nitrates</u>

- <u>Cycloserine</u>

- <u>Antidiabetic agents</u> including insulin and sulfonylureas (due to risk of hypoglycemia)

- Any other drug which, based upon a pharmacist's professional judgment, may pose a substantial risk to the person consuming the drug when taken in combination with alcohol

## CHILD-RESISTANT PACKAGING

Before the implementation of the Poison Prevention Packaging Act (PPPA), accidental poison exposure was a leading cause of injury in children less than 5 years old. There was no standard way to protect children from ingesting common dangerous substances, including drugs and household chemicals. The PPPA, which is enforced by the Consumer Product Safety Commission, requires the use of child-resistant (C-R) containers for most over-the-counter drugs, prescription drugs, and household chemicals.

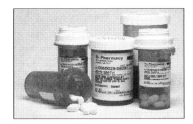

C-R containers are designed so that 80% of children less than 5 years of age cannot open it while at least 90% of adults can. The PPPA mandates that <u>a new plastic container and closure</u> (top) must be used for <u>each prescription dispensed</u>. This is done to avoid wear and tear damage, which can reduce the C-R effectiveness of the container. If a glass container is used, only the top plastic closure needs to be replaced. Reversible containers (child-resistant when turning the closure in one direction, but not child-resistant in the other direction) are permitted if dispensed in the child-resistant mode, but are not recommended.

---

73  *CCR 1744(b)*

The patient or the prescriber can ask the pharmacy to package prescription drugs in an "easy open" container that is not child-resistant. The <u>prescriber</u> can waive the use of a C-R container for a <u>single</u> prescription at a time, and the <u>patient can provide a blanket waiver</u> for all dispensed prescriptions at a pharmacy. The pharmacist should document the waiver request with the patient's signature.

For the benefit of elderly and handicapped patients who might have difficulty opening C-R containers, the PPPA allow manufacturers to package one size of an OTC product in a non-compliant "easy open" container as long as the same product is also available in a C-R container. The non-compliant container must carry a warning that it is not recommended for use in households with children.

C-R packaging requirements do not apply if the drug is to be administered directly by a healthcare provider to an institutionalized patient.

## DRUG UTILIZATION REVIEW

There are two types of drug utilization reviews (DUR) required for the pharmacist and/or state to perform:

- <u>Prospective DUR</u>: an evaluation of a patient's medication profile <u>prior</u> to dispensing, performed by the <u>dispensing</u> pharmacist every time a prescription is filled.[74] This is done to look for therapeutic duplication, incorrect dosing, incorrect treatment duration, contraindications, interactions between drug/disease state, allergies, or signs of abuse or diversion. The requirement to perform a prospective DUR is the reason why the clerk at the window asks the patient if they have any new medications or allergies; if so, these will be added to the profile, and the pharmacist will review the current use and the condition of the patient in order to confirm, each time, that the drug is safe to dispense.

- <u>Retrospective DUR</u>: a review of drug therapy <u>after</u> the drug is dispensed. These are typically conducted for many patients at one time, and are required by the state (according to the Omnibus Budget Reconciliation Act), by a medical institution (such as a hospital) or by an insurance company. Retrospective reviews are used to detect and correct inappropriate prescribing patterns, or the presence of fraud or abuse.

_74   CCR 1707.3_

## PATIENT MEDICATION PROFILES

A pharmacy must keep medication profiles on all patients who have prescriptions filled at the pharmacy <u>except</u> when the pharmacist feels that the patient <u>will not come back to the pharmacy</u>. For example, a patient from another state or foreign country visiting California for a vacation can fill a prescription at a local pharmacy, but is unlikely to return. In most cases, patients do return and a profile is required. The following information must be kept on a patient profile:[75]

- The patient's full name and address, telephone number, date of birth (or age) and gender.

- For each prescription dispensed by the pharmacy:

  - The name, strength, dosage form, route of administration (if other than oral), quantity and directions

  - The prescriber's name and license number, and if needed, the DEA registration number or other unique identifier

  - The date each drug was dispensed or refilled

  - The prescription number for each prescription

- Any of the following which can relate to drug therapy: patient allergies, idiosyncrasies, current medications and relevant prior medications, including OTC medications, devices, or medical conditions, if provided.

- Any other information which the pharmacist, in his or her professional judgment, feels is appropriate to include.

The patient medication record must be kept for at least <u>one year</u> from the date when the last prescription was filled.

## WRITTEN PATIENT INFORMATION

There are three types of written information that can be provided to the patient:

- Consumer Medication Information (CMI) leaflets

- Patient Package Inserts (PPIs)

- Medication Guides (MedGuides)

75   CCR 1707.1

## Consumer Medication Information

The FDA requires pharmacies to provide useful written patient information to patients with each <u>new</u> prescription. This is provided as consumer medication information (CMI) leaflets. Unlike PPIs and MedGuides (described below), CMIs are not reviewed or approved by the FDA. The CMIs are usually placed inside the prescription bag or stapled to the outside. The purpose of the CMI is to supplement oral counseling and provide basic information on how to use the drug and what to expect.

## Patient Package Inserts

The widespread use of patient package inserts (PPIs) began with the use of estrogen-containing birth control pills. Oral contraceptives were first available in 1960 and, at that time, the estrogen dose in the contraceptives was much higher than the doses used currently. Consequently, there was a higher incidence of venous thromboembolism (VTE, or "clotting"). Oral contraceptives quickly became very popular, and many women were using them without any awareness of the clotting risk. In order for the patient to be informed of the benefits and risks, the FDA required pharmacies to provide a PPI to patients whenever estrogen-containing drugs are dispensed. The PPIs, as part of the drug's labeling, are <u>approved by the FDA</u>.

Although the estrogen content in oral contraceptives is lower in the common formulations used today, PPIs must still be given <u>each time</u> an estrogen-containing drug is dispensed in the <u>outpatient setting</u>, regardless of whether it is an initial fill or refill. In an <u>institutionalized setting</u>, such as a hospital or long-term care facility, the PPI must be provided to the patient <u>before the administration of the first dose</u> and <u>every 30 days</u> thereafter.[76] Due to clotting risk, the use of estrogen in long-term care facilities is unlikely, but the legal requirement remains. If the PPI is not provided when appropriate, it is considered misbranding.

---

*76   21 CFR 310.515*

## Medication Guides

Medication Guides (MedGuides) are FDA-approved patient handouts that come with many prescription medications that have <u>significant health concerns</u>. The FDA requires that MedGuides be issued with drugs and biologics that require information to help prevent serious ADRs, if the patient needs to know about serious side effects or ADRs, or if adherence to specific instructions is essential to the drug's effectiveness. The manufacturer must supply the MedGuides to the pharmacy by providing the physical handouts or the electronic file so the pharmacy can print them out for the patient.

The MedGuide must be given in each of the following situations:[77]

- <u>Every time</u> (initial fill and refills) the drug is dispensed in the <u>outpatient setting</u>, and when the drug will be used by the patient without the supervision of a healthcare provider

- The <u>first time</u> the drug is being dispensed to a healthcare provider for <u>administration</u> to a patient in an outpatient setting (e.g., in a clinic, an infusion center, or emergency department)

- When the patient or their caregiver asks for it

- If the MedGuide has been revised

- If the drug is subject to a Risk Evaluation and Mitigation Strategy (REMS), which requires a MedGuide

There are over 240 medications which require MedGuides, the list can be found on the FDA website.[78] Drug classes that require MedGuides include <u>antidepressants, some antipsychotics, anticonvulsants, long-acting beta agonists, most antiarrhythmics and NSAIDs</u>. The health issues associated with the drug are described in the RxPrep Course Book.

---

77   http://www.fda.gov/downloads/Drugs/.../Guidances/UCM244570.pdf (accessed 2018 Feb 16).
78   http://www.fda.gov/Drugs/DrugSafety/ucm085729.htm (accessed 2018 Feb 16).

## SELECT DRUGS WITH MEDGUIDES

**Antidepressants**
Bupropion (*Wellbutrin*)

Citalopram (*Celexa*)

Doxepin (*Sinequan*)

Duloxetine (*Cymbalta*)

Escitalopram (*Lexapro*)

Fluoxetine (*Prozac*)

Imipramine (*Tofranil*)

Mirtazapine (*Remeron*)

Nortriptyline (*Pamelor*)

Paroxetine (*Paxil*)

Sertraline (*Zoloft*)

Trazodone (*Desyrel*)

Venlafaxine (*Effexor*)

**Insomnia**
Eszopiclone (*Lunesta*)

Ramelteon (*Rozerem*)

Temazepam (*Restoril*)

Triazolam (*Halcion*)

Zaleplon (*Sonata*)

Zolpidem (*Ambien*)

**ADHD Drugs**
Atomoxetine (*Strattera*)

Dexmethylphenidate (*Focalin*)

Dextroamphetamine (*Dexedrine*)

Dextroamphetamine/Amphetamine (*Adderall*)

Lisdexamfetamine (*Vyvanse*)

Methylphenidate (*Concerta, Daytrana, Metadate CD, Methylin, Ritalin*)

**Antipsychotics**
Aripiprazole (*Abilify*)

Quetiapine (*Seroquel*)

**Retinoids**
Acitretin (*Soriatane*)

Isotretinoin (*Absorica, Amnesteem, Claravis, Myorisan, Zenatane*)

**NSAIDS**
Celecoxib (*Celebrex*)

Diclofenac (*Voltaren, Flector, Cambia*)

Diclofenac/misoprostol (*Arthrotec*)

Etodolac

Ibuprofen (*Advil, Motrin*)

Ibuprofen/hydrocodone (*Vicoprofen*)

Indomethacin (*Indocin*)

Ketorolac (*SPRIX*)

Meloxicam (*Mobic*)

Nabumetone

Naproxen (*Aleve, Naprosyn, Anaprox*)

Oxaprozin (*Daypro*)

**Long-Acting Beta Agonists**
Arformoterol (*Brovana*)

Formoterol (*Foradil Aerolizer, Perforomist*)

Formoterol/budesonide (*Symbicort*)

Salmeterol (*Serevent Diskus*)

Salmeterol/fluticasone (*Advair Diskus, Advair HFA*)

**Diabetes Drugs**
Exenatide (*Bydureon, Byetta*)

Pioglitazone (*Actos*)

Pioglitazone/metformin (*Actoplus Met*)

Rosiglitazone (*Avandia*)

Rosiglitazone/metformin (*Avandamet*)

**Antiarrhythmics**
Amiodarone (*Cordarone, Pacerone*)

**Others**
Bupropion (*Zyban*)

Fentanyl (*Duragesic, Fentora*)

Pimecrolimus (*Elidel*)

Raloxifene (*Evista*)

Tacrolimus (*Protopic, Prograf, Astagraf*)

Tamoxifen (*Soltamox*)

Teriparatide (*Forteo*)

Testosterone (*Androgel*)

Varenicline (*Chantix*)

Warfarin (*Coumadin, Jantoven*)

## RISK EVALUATION AND MITIGATION STRATEGY

The Food and Drug Administration Amendments Act of 2007 gave the FDA the authority to require a Risk Evaluation and Mitigation Strategy (REMS) from manufacturers to ensure that the benefits of certain drugs or biologics outweigh its risks. If the FDA feels that the drug has very high safety concerns that would not be sufficiently addressed with the use of boxed warnings and MedGuides, the FDA can mandate the use of a REMS. The FDA uses the REMS requirements to make sure that the risks are known and are managed adequately.[79] There are four parts to a REMS:

- Communication plans
- Implementation systems
- Elements to assure safe use (ETASU)
- MedGuides

Since the safety issues are different with each drug, the REMS will need to be different. These are examples of REMS requirements for certain drugs:

| DRUG | RISK | REMS |
| --- | --- | --- |
| Thalidomide | Severe birth defects | *Thalomid* REMS Program (previously called the STEPS Program)[80] Negative pregnancy test required prior to dispensing each prescription. |
| Isotretinoin | Severe birth defects | iPledge Program[81] Negative pregnancy test required prior to dispensing each prescription. |
| Clozapine | Neutropenia | Clozapine REMS program Monitor the absolute neutrophil count (ANC). |
| *Qsymia* | Severe birth defects | *Qsymia* REMS Program[82] MedGuide required, healthcare training program, dispensed through certified pharmacies only. |
| *Avinza, Butrans, Dolophine, Duragesic, Exalgo, Hysingla ER, Kadian, Methadose, MS Contin, Nucynta ER, Oxycontin, Zohydro ER, Hysingla,* and all other ER/LA opioid analgesics | High abuse potential, life-threatening respiratory depression | ER/LA Opioid Analgesics REMS Program[83] MedGuide required, and prescribers must complete approved CE and must counsel patients |
| *Saxenda* | Potential risk of medullary thyroid carcinoma, risk of acute pancreatitis | *Saxenda* REMS Program[84] |
| *Addyi* | Risk of hypotension and syncope due to an interaction with alcohol | *Addyi* REMS Program No alcohol use while taking *Addyi*. All REMS participants must be trained and patients must be properly counseled. |

79  http://www.accessdata.fda.gov/scripts/cder/rems/index.cfm (accessed 2018 Feb 16).
80  http://www.thalomidrems.com/ (accessed 2018 Feb 16).
81  https://www.ipledgeprogram.com/ (accessed 2018 Feb 16).
82  http://www.qsymiarems.com/ (accessed 2018 Feb 16).
83  http://www.er-la-opioidrems.com/ (accessed 2018 Feb 16).
84  http://www.saxendarems.com/ (accessed 2018 Feb 16).

## PATIENT COUNSELING

Pharmacists must provide counseling (oral consultation) in any of the following situations:[85]

- The prescription drug has not been previously dispensed to the patient

- The refill is being dispensed in a different dosage form, strength, or with a new written prescription

- If the patient requests counseling

- When the pharmacist feels counseling is necessary

The patient counseling must include at least the following items:[86]

- <u>Directions for use and storage</u>

- The <u>importance of compliance with directions</u>

- <u>Precautions and relevant warnings</u>, including common, severe side or adverse effects, and interactions that can be encountered.

When the pharmacist feels it is necessary, the patient counseling can also include:[87]

- The name and a description of the drug

- The route of administration

- The dose and/or the dosage form

- The duration of therapy

- Any special directions for use and storage

- Instructions on how to prepare the drug for administration

- Techniques for self-monitoring

- Refill information

- Additional adverse drug reactions or interactions

- What to do if a dose is missed

85   CCR 1707.2
86   CCR 1707.2(c)
87   CCR 1707.2(d)

Only the <u>pharmacist</u> or <u>intern pharmacist</u> can make the <u>offer to counsel</u>. Although the offer to counsel must be made, the patient or patient's caregiver can refuse counseling. The pharmacist provides patient counseling in an area suitable for <u>confidential patient consultation</u> to protect the patient's protected health information.

If the prescription is <u>mailed</u> or delivered, there must be a <u>written notice</u> that a pharmacist is available if the patient has any questions and a telephone number that the patient can call.[88]

Pharmacies often interact with patients with a limited grasp of the English language, and all patients need to know how to safely use their medications. In California, pharmacies are required to provide <u>interpretive services</u> in the patient's language during all hours that the pharmacy is open, either in person by the pharmacy staff who can communicate in the patient's language, or by the use of a third-party interpretive service available by telephone that is at or close to the pharmacy counter.[89] Communication concerns are discussed in the RxPrep Course Book chapter on Patient Charts, Assessment & Healthcare Provider Communication.

Pharmacists are not required by state law to counsel inpatients; however, pharmacists must provide discharge counseling.[90]

## NOTICE TO CONSUMERS

The purpose of the <u>Notice to Consumers</u> is to make sure consumers understand that they <u>have certain rights</u>, which includes the requirement to <u>receive counseling from a pharmacist</u> with each new prescription, the type of information that should be provided, and the patient's <u>right to ask questions</u> about their medications. The notice advises the patient that <u>easy-to-read type</u> and <u>interpretive services</u> are available on request. The full-size poster of the "Notice to Consumers" must be posted in <u>public view</u> where it can be read by the consumer. The posters can be ordered on the board's website. Smaller versions can be printed out on legal size paper. The poster can be provided in languages that most apply to the pharmacy's customer population. Alternatively, written receipts containing the required information can be provided to patients. This is an acceptable option for settings in which the patient does not physically see the pharmacist, such as mail-order or closed-door pharmacies. A pharmacy can also opt to display a PowerPoint presentation of the notice on a videoscreen.

---

88  CCR 1707.2(b)(2)
89  CCR 1707.5(d)
90  B&PC 4074(e)

# Point to your language.
## Interpreter services will be provided to you upon request at no cost.

| | | | |
|---|---|---|---|
| **ARABIC** | اختر لغتك.<br><br>يتم تقديم خدمات الترجمة الفورية لك عند الطلب دون أي تكلفة . | Ն2եք ձեր լեզուն։<br><br>Թարգմանչի ծառայությունները անվճար կտրամադրվեն ձեզ՝ ըստ պահանջի։ | **ARMENIAN** |
| **CAMBODIAN** | ចូរចង្អុលទៅកាន់ភាសារបស់អ្នក ។<br><br>មានផ្ដល់សេវាកម្មបកប្រែភាសាជូនអ្នក តាមការស្នើសុំ ដោយឥតគិតថ្លៃ ។ | 廣州話<br>指向您的語言。<br><br>將根據您的要求免費為您提供翻譯服務。 | **CANTONESE** |
| **FARSI** | زبان خود را مشخص کنید.<br><br>خدمات ترجمه شفاهی بر حسب درخواست شما به صورت رایگان فراهم خواهد شد. | Taw rau koj yam lus.<br><br>Kev pab cuam neeg txhais lus yuav muaj pub rau koj raws li kev thov yam tsis yuav nqi. | **HMONG** |
| **KOREAN** | 언어를 지정해 주십시오.<br><br>요청 시 통역 서비스를 무료로 제공해 드립니다. | 官話<br>指向您的语言。<br><br>将根据您的要求免费为您提供翻译服务。 | **MANDARIN** |
| **RUSSIAN** | Указать на ваш язык.<br><br>Услуги переводчика будут бесплатно предоставлены Вам по требованию. | Indique su idioma.<br><br>Se le proporcionarán servicios de intérprete sin costo si lo solicita. | **SPANISH** |
| **TAGALOG** | Ituro ang iyong wika.<br><br>Ang serbisyo ng interpreter ay ibibigay sa iyo kapag hihilingin nang walang bayad. | Xin hãy chỉ vào ngôn ngữ của quý vị.<br><br>Dịch vụ thông dịch sẽ được cung cấp cho quý vị miễn phí theo yêu cầu. | **VIETNAMESE** |

Image courtesy of the California Board of Pharmacy

# Ask Your Pharmacist!

## You have the right to ask the pharmacist for:

California law requires a pharmacist to speak with you every time you get a **new** prescription.

Before taking your medicine, be sure you know:

**1** The name of the medicine and what it does.

**2** How and when to take it, for how long, and what to do if you miss a dose.

**3** Possible side effects and what you should do if they occur.

**4** Whether the new medicine will work safely with other medicines or supplements.

**5** What foods, drinks, or activities should be avoided while taking the medicine.

### Easy-to-read type
You have the right to ask for and receive from any pharmacy prescription drug labels in 12-point font.

### Interpreter services
Interpreter services are available to you upon request at no cost.

### Drug pricing
You may ask this pharmacy for information on drug pricing and use of generic drugs.

## Ask the pharmacist if you have any questions.

This pharmacy must provide any medicine or device legally prescribed for you, unless:

- It is not covered by your insurance;
- You are unable to pay the cost of a copayment;
- The pharmacist determines doing so would be against the law or potentially harmful to health.

If a medicine or device is not immediately available, the pharmacy will work with you to help you get your medicine or device in a timely manner.

**BE AWARE AND TAKE CARE:**
Talk to your pharmacist!
CALIFORNIA STATE BOARD OF PHARMACY

1625 N. Market Blvd., Suite N-219 • Sacramento, CA 95834
(916) 574-7900 • www.pharmacy.ca.gov

Image courtesy of the California Board of Pharmacy

## THE HEALTH INSURANCE PORTABILITY AND ACCOUNTABILITY ACT

The Health Insurance Portability and Accountability Act (HIPAA) contains privacy protection provisions that apply to health information created or stored by healthcare providers who engage in electronic transactions and work with healthcare providers and health plans.

The standards for privacy outlined in HIPAA are called the "privacy rule." The standards outline the requirements to protect the privacy of a patient's health information, how it can be shared, and provides the patient the right to access their own information. The goal in designing the rule was to protect the individuals' health information, while allowing the flow of data needed to provide high quality healthcare. All healthcare professionals who have access to confidential patient health information (PHI) must have documented HIPAA training. Violation of HIPAA, either inadvertently or deliberately, can result in fines as high as $50,000 per violation and imprisonment up to 10 years.[91] An individual at each facility must be designated to enforce the privacy policy.

The information covered under HIPAA is called <u>protected health information</u> and includes private information in electronic, verbal, or written form. According to HIPAA, PHI includes:

- The patient's past, present, or future <u>physical or mental health or condition</u> (e.g., medical record)

- The <u>healthcare provided</u> to the patient (e.g., laboratory tests, surgery)

- The past, present, or future <u>payment</u> for providing healthcare to the patient, which can identify the patient. (e.g., hospital bill)

Protected health information includes many common identifiers, such as the name, address, birth date and social security number when they can be associated with the health information listed above. If the identifying information is not related to health information, then it is not considered PHI. For example, names, residential addresses, or phone numbers listed in a public directory such as a phone book would not be PHI because there is no health data associated with it.

The healthcare facility or pharmacy must ensure that any patient information is secure and not available to viewers who do not require access. Healthcare providers must be mindful to:

- Avoid discussing patient care in elevators

- Shred all patient health documents prior to disposal

- Cover patient identifiers on prescription bottles and bags prior and during dispensing

- Close patient records on computer screens when not in use and logout of the system

---

91 http://www.hhs.gov/hipaa/for-professionals/privacy/laws-regulations/index.html (accessed 2018 Feb 16).

Examples of HIPAA violations include:

- Prescription labels with patient identifiers in the regular trash

- Pharmacy employees looking around in celebrity patient records for non-work purposes

- Pictures or heath records about patients posted on social media sites

The "minimum necessary" information required for the job is what should be shared. This becomes an issue for pharmacists when the insurer may not wish to pay without additional information, which the pharmacist may not think is required. The terminology of "minimum necessary" is designed to encourage the staff to evaluate who should be accessing patient records. If the support staff do not need patient medical records to do their jobs, they should not have access. A pharmacy student accessing a relative's medical records at a hospital during their intern experience (when they are not involved with the relative's medical care at the facility) would constitute a privacy violation.

It is permissible to share PHI with:

- The patient

- Other healthcare providers providing care to the patient

- For treatment, payment, or operation (TPO) purposes

- Other persons when authorized by the patient

- As part of a limited data set for research, public health or institutional operations

- For a public health need (including natural emergencies), drug abuse issues for law enforcement, the DEA, medical board inspectors, pharmacy board inspectors, or to report adverse drug reactions to the FDA

If the release of PHI is not for TPO purposes, the pharmacist must receive the patient's written authorization prior to the release. This authorization must include whom the information will be shared with, the purpose, the expiration date, and the patient's signature. If the patient is requesting the release, a written authorization is not necessary, but some facilities will require it. The facility will have the patient sign a form that they have received the HIPAA paperwork in order to document compliance.

Incidental disclosures are not a HIPAA violation; such as being accidentally overheard when counseling a patient at a pharmacy, or when discussing a patient's care during medical rounds. When the pharmacy staff needs to have the patient come to the pharmacy counter, the staff member should say "Mr. Jones, please return to the pharmacy" instead of "Mr. Jones, your *Seroquel* is ready for pick up." When the pharmacy needs to leave a voicemail, the staff member should ask the patient to call the pharmacy back only, and not mention the medication name. Prescriptions can be picked up by family or friends unless the pharmacist has reason to believe that this would be against the wishes of the patient.

HIPAA requires a site-specific notice of privacy practices to protect patient information and to make known whom it may be shared with. This should be in simple language, and state the patient's rights to receive their own information. The privacy notice should make clear that any release beyond that which is stated in the policy will require the patient's approval. It should list the contact for Department of Health & Human Services (DHHS) if the patient wishes to file a complaint concerning HIPAA violations, along with the contact for a person within the pharmacy if the patient wishes to discuss privacy concerns.

The privacy notice must be given to the patient on the first day that service is provided. The pharmacy must make a good faith effort to obtain the patient's written acknowledgment that they have received the privacy notice. The pharmacy cannot deny service if the patient refuses to sign; if this occurs, the pharmacy should document the patient's refusal to sign. The written acknowledgment that the patient received the privacy notice must be separate from other signatures obtained by the pharmacy, such as signing for the prescriptions received. The privacy notice should also be placed in a prominent location within the pharmacy and on the pharmacy's website.

The patient has the right to obtain a copy of their records. In California, patients must be able to inspect their medical records within five business days of making a written request, and receive copies within 15 business days. The maximum charge for copies is $0.25 cents/page, or $0.50 cents/page if the copies are being made from microfilm, plus the addition of reasonable clerical costs incurred in making the records available.[92] The patient can request a copy in the format of their choice (such as a printed copy or an electronic version sent via email).

---

92  *H&SC 123110*

## DRUG SUBSTITUTION AND SELECTION

### Substituting Brand for Generic and the *Orange Book*

The FDA publishes and frequently updates the *Approved Drug Products with Therapeutic Equivalence Evaluations* (commonly known as the *Orange Book*), which serves as a guide for therapeutically equivalent drugs. A pharmacist can select another drug with the same active chemical ingredients with the same strength, quantity, and dosage form, and with the same generic drug name as determined by the United States Adopted Names (USAN), and accepted by the FDA. Generally, the substitutions are made according to the *Orange Book 's* therapeutic equivalence ratings (see box).

| A202266 | AB | No | CLOPIDOGREL BISULFATE | TABLET; ORAL | EQ 300MG BASE | CLOPIDOGREL BISULFATE | WOCKHARDT LTD |
|---|---|---|---|---|---|---|---|
| A202266 | AB | No | CLOPIDOGREL BISULFATE | TABLET; ORAL | EQ 75MG BASE | CLOPIDOGREL BISULFATE | WOCKHARDT LTD |
| A201686 | AB | No | CLOPIDOGREL BISULFATE | TABLET; ORAL | EQ 75MG BASE | CLOPIDOGREL BISULFATE | ZYDUS PHARMS USA INC |
| N020839 | AB | Yes | CLOPIDOGREL BISULFATE | TABLET; ORAL | EQ 300MG BASE | PLAVIX | SANOFI AVENTIS US |
| N020839 | AB | No | CLOPIDOGREL BISULFATE | TABLET; ORAL | EQ 75MG BASE | PLAVIX | SANOFI AVENTIS US |

The purpose of substitution is to provide the patient with a lower cost drug; thus, the product that is substituted cannot cost more than the brand. When a substitution is made, the cost-savings from the switch must be <u>communicated to the patient</u>. If the generic equivalent is dispensed, the generic name, the statement "generic for _____" where the brand name is inserted, and the manufacturer name must be on the label (e.g., atorvastatin, generic for *Lipitor*, MFR: *Mylan Pharmaceuticals*). If the brand is dispensed, only the brand name is required on the label since the brand name is registered to the manufacturer.

A substitution cannot be made if the prescriber has taken any of the following actions:[93]

- Indicates, either orally, in handwriting or electronically "Do not substitute."

- Checks off a box pre-printed with the text "Do not substitute."

- Initials a box pre-printed with the text "Do not substitute."

The *Orange Book* is available in print, as an online version from the FDA website[94] or by using a mobile application to access the *Orange Book Express*.

> ### THERAPEUTIC EQUIVALENCE AND THE *ORANGE BOOK*
>
> The Orange Book uses a two-letter code system to indicate whether or not a generic drug is therapeutically equivalent to the branded drug.
>
> If the <u>first letter is A</u>, such as in an AB rated drug, the generic is <u>therapeutically equivalent</u> to the reference listed drug (RLD), which is the branded drug that the generic was compared to in studies that the generic manufacturer submitted to the FDA.
>
> If the <u>first letter is B</u>, such as in a BB rated drug, the formulation is <u>not therapeutically equivalent</u>.
>
> The second letter indicates the route of administration or the formulation, such as in an AT rated drug where the A indicates equivalence to the RLD, and the T indicates that it is a topical formulation.

93   B&PC 4073(b)
94   www.fda.gov/cder/ob/default.htm (accessed 2018 Feb 20).

## Substituting Drug Formulations

### Switching the Formulation

A pharmacist can select a <u>different formulation</u> with the <u>same active ingredients</u> of <u>equivalent strength and duration of therapy</u> as the prescribed drug when the change will <u>improve patient compliance</u>. For example, if a pharmacist gets a prescription for 1/2 of the single strength sulfamethoxazole/trimethoprim tablets for a child, the pharmacist may suggest a 5 mL/dose of the pediatric suspension to the child's parents. If the prescriber has indicated that no drug substitution is allowed, the formulation should not be changed.[95]

### Formulations That Cannot be Switched

Substitution is <u>not permitted</u> between <u>long-acting</u> and <u>short-acting forms</u> of a medication with the same chemical ingredients. For example, the long-acting form of clonidine that is indicated for ADHD (*Kapvay*) cannot be interchanged with immediate-release clonidine.

Substitution is also <u>not permitted</u> between <u>combination drug products</u> and <u>multiple single-agents</u>.[96] For example, it would not be permissible to exchange the combination drug isosorbide dinitrate/hydralazine (*BiDil*) to the two individual drugs as separate products.

---

95   *B&PC 4052.5(a-b)*
96   *B&PC 4052.5 (f)*

## Substituting Biological Products and the *Purple Book*

<u>Biologics</u> are created from living organisms by programming cell lines to produce the desired therapeutic substances. Biologics are complex, large molecular compounds. In contrast, most other drugs are produced chemically and are smaller, simpler compounds with precise structures. Due to the complexity of biologics, it is difficult to create a true interchangeable product.[97] The original brand name biologic product is referred to as the <u>reference product</u>. A <u>biosimilar</u> is a biological product that has <u>highly similar</u> structure and function to the reference product and has no significant difference in <u>safety</u> and <u>effectiveness</u> from the reference product. The biosimilar for filgrastim (*Neupogen*) is filgrastim-sndz (*Zarxio*), and the biosimilar for infliximab (*Remicade*) is infliximab-dyyb (*Inflectra*).[98] A biosimilar product is <u>not automatically interchangeable</u> with the reference product. The biosimilar must prove that it would have the <u>same clinical effect</u> as the reference product in any given patient in order to be considered <u>interchangeable</u>.[99]

The *Lists of Licensed Biological Products with Reference Product Exclusivity and Biosimilarity or Interchangeability Evaluations* (commonly referred to as *The Purple Book*) lists the reference products, biosimilar products, and interchangeable products.

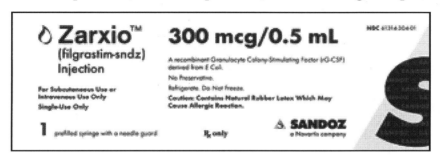

*The package label for Zarxio, the first drug approved as a biosimilar in the U.S.*

Pharmacists can dispense an interchangeable biosimilar product in place of the prescribed reference product, unless the prescriber indicates otherwise. The dispensed biosimilar product <u>cannot cost more</u> than the prescribed biological product and the substitution must be communicated to the patient.[100] The biosimilar will cost less than the original biologic product, but will still be costly due to the complexity involved with manufacturing these types of drugs.

When a biosimilar has been dispensed in place of the prescribed biological product, the pharmacist or someone they designate must <u>make an entry into an electronic record</u> of the specific product provided to the patient, including the name of the biologic and the manufacturer. This entry will need to be <u>accessible to the prescriber</u> through a medical records system, through a pharmacy benefit management system, or through some type of electronic prescribing system. If such a system is not available, the pharmacist will need to <u>notify the prescriber</u> directly with the specific product dispensed.

97   http://www.fda.gov/AboutFDA/CentersOffices/OfficeofMedicalProductsandTobacco/CBER/ucm133077.htm (accessed 2018 Feb 16),
98   http://www.fda.gov/NewsEvents/Newsroom/PressAnnouncements/ucm494227.htm (accessed 2018 Feb 16).
99   https://www.fda.gov/drugs/developmentapprovalprocess/howdrugsaredevelopedandapproved/approvalapplications/therapeuticbiologicapplications/biosimilars/ucm411418.htm (accessed 2018 Feb 16).
100  B&PC 4073.5

## Drug Formularies

A formulary is a preferred drug list that a hospital or other institution, healthcare plan, or pharmacy benefit manager (PBM) has chosen for their patients or members. The formulary should include the <u>safest</u> and <u>most effective</u> drugs according to current clinical guidelines/ practices, while taking <u>cost</u> into consideration. When similar drugs exist in a class, a competitive bidding process is used. For example, if a pharmacy and therapeutics (P&T) committee wishes to select a prostaglandin analogue for glaucoma, and there are five equally safe and effective agents on the market, the committee is likely to choose the least expensive option.

The P&T committee is responsible for managing the drug formulary, managing the therapeutic interchange protocol, conducting medication/drug use evaluation (MUE/DUE), monitoring/ reporting adverse drug reactions, medication-error safety initiatives, and developing clinical care plans and guidelines within an organization (e.g., hospital, pharmacy benefit management). The P&T members include physicians, pharmacists, nurses, administrators, quality improvement managers, and other healthcare professionals.

Healthcare plans have formularies to outline which drugs will be covered in the outpatient or retail setting. Patients can refer to these formularies to be aware of different tiers and copays. The typical formulary for outpatient use has 3, 4, or 5 tiers. The lower tier level has a lower copay. A copay is the out-of-pocket expense that the patient is responsible for in order to receive services such as doctors visits and prescription drugs. Specialty drugs, including the biologics, will be placed on a high tier (such as tier 4 or 5) and may require prior authorization from the insurance plan in order to permit the patient to obtain the drug using the insurance coverage.

An example of formulary drug tiers for outpatient prescription medications:

| TIER | TIER NAME | COST TO PATIENT (COPAY) |
|------|-----------|-------------------------|
| 1 | Generic drugs | $5 per prescription |
| 2 | Preferred brand drugs | $15 per prescription |
| 3 | Non-preferred brand drugs | $25 per prescription |
| 4 | Specialty drugs | 10% copay, up to $250 maximum per prescription |

If a drug has a history of unsafe use, it may be withdrawn from the formulary. If there are sound-alike, look-alike drugs, the P&T committee may remove one of them to avoid mix-ups. If multiple drugs have similar risk-benefit profiles, it is likely the least expensive drug will be included and the pricier drug will be excluded. Or, if one agent has safety risks but is effective in refractory cases, it can be given restricted-use status and can be used only if the patient has failed the first-line agents.

### Therapeutic Interchange Protocol

Therapeutic interchange is the dispensing of medications by pharmacists that are chemically different, but therapeutically similar, to the medication prescribed. The drug that is substituted is usually in the same pharmacological/therapeutic class. Most hospitals, nursing facilities and other healthcare institutions have therapeutic interchange protocols as a cost-effective strategy: a new and more expensive drug can be interchanged with an older, less costly drug that provides a similar therapeutic benefit. Therapeutic interchange has become much more common in recent years because of many drugs in the same therapeutic class. The P&T committee (which consists of pharmacists, physicians, and other healthcare providers) will determine which drugs should be included in the institution's therapeutic interchange protocol.

The pharmacist who substitutes one drug for another does not need to discuss the change with a physician as long as the substitution is established in the institution's therapeutic interchange protocol. For example, if rosuvastatin (*Crestor*) is not on the formulary but the generic atorvastatin and simvastatin are on the formulary, the hospital pharmacist will choose the therapeutically equivalent dose of a formulary drug when *Crestor* is ordered by the physician. The agents most commonly included on therapeutic interchange programs are antacids, H2-blockers, hypnotics, ACE inhibitors, angiotensin receptor blockers, proton pump inhibitors, potassium supplements, quinolones, first, second and third-generation cephalosporins, statins, insulins, topical steroids and laxatives and stool softeners.

Example of therapeutic equivalence: For all other PPIs, use pantoprazole 40 mg.

Example of IV to PO (can be written as IV:PO) conversion: For levofloxacin IV to treat a mild-moderate infection in a patient consuming a normal diet (not NPO), use the same dose of oral levofloxacin (e.g., 500 or 250 mg).

Therapeutic interchange can also be used in ambulatory practice settings as long as the two basic requirements exist: the presence of a functioning formulary system and a P&T committee.

## AUTOMATED DRUG DELIVERY SYSTEMS

Automated drug delivery systems (ADDS) are cabinets that are used to store and dispense drugs to patients in skilled nursing and intermediate care facilities, hospital units, and sometimes in other locations, such as medical clinics. An ADDS can also be referred to as an automated dispensing system (ADS) or an automated dispensing cabinet (ADC).

This section focuses on the use of the cabinets in skilled nursing or intermediate care facilities due to the lack of a pharmacy in most of these facilities, and the risk of diversion. If a patient is discharged or passes away, or has a change of medication, unused drug can be diverted. If the ADDS is used to store and dispense scheduled drugs, a DEA-registered pharmacy must manage the cabinet. The California board of pharmacy requires that the system be under the control of a pharmacist and specifies how the cabinet should be stocked.

For systems located in a skilled or intermediate care facility, the following is required:[101]

■ The pharmacy and the nursing facility have developed P&Ps to ensure that the drugs are being stored and dispensed properly.

■ The pharmacist reviews each medication order and the patient's profile before the drug is removed from the ADDS. Use of an override to retrieve medication before the pharmacist can review the order should be done in emergency situations only.

■ When the cabinet is stocked directly in the facility, the stocking is done by a pharmacist.

■ If the ADDS uses removable pockets, drawers, or similar technology, the stocking is done outside the facility (at the pharmacy) and delivered back to the facility. With this type of stocking, the removable pockets or drawers must be transported between the pharmacy and the facility in a secure, tamper-evident container, and once the removable pockets or drawers are brought back to the pharmacy, they are restocked by a pharmacist or by an intern pharmacist or technician working under the supervision of a pharmacist.

The board is also concerned that drugs stored in an ADDS are properly labeled. The drugs must be labeled with at least the following information: name of drug, strength and dosage form, manufacturer and manufacturer's lot number, and expiration date.

Pharmacies that remotely operate an ADDS must register the ADDS with the board within 30 days of installing the device and annually as part of license renewal. The pharmacy also has to inform the board in writing if the pharmacy discontinues operating the ADDS.[102] This includes pharmacies that remotely operate ADDS in long-term care facilities. Hospitals that operate ADDS within their own facility do not need to register the ADDS separately with the board.[103]

101   H&SC 1261.6
102   B&PC 4105.5 (b)
103   B&PC 4105.5 (e)

## REPACKAGING

### Repackaging Drugs in Anticipation of Receiving Prescriptions

Drugs can be pre-counted or poured (repackaged) from a stock container (which is large) into smaller quantities suitable for dispensing. This is often done for fast-movers so that the commonly dispensed drugs can be filled and dispensed quickly once the prescription is received, and for drugs that are not available at a reasonable cost in smaller quantities, or for drugs that do not come as unit dose and are needed as unit dose for a hospital or other type of institutional setting.

The repackaging should be done according to the Current Good Manufacturing Practices (CGMPs), and the drugs must be properly labeled with at least the following information: name of drug, strength, dosage form, manufacturer's name and lot number, expiration date, and quantity per repackaged unit. If the approved labeling contains instructions for handling or storage of the product, the repackaging will need to be done in accordance with those instructions. Otherwise, it would be considered to be in conflict with the approved labeling. A log is kept for drugs pre-packed for future dispensing.

### Repackaging Previously Dispensed Drugs into Blister Packs

Drugs previously dispensed can be repackaged at the patient's request into a package that is more convenient for the patient.[104] This type of packaging is referred to as a "medication blister pack" or "bubble blister pack" or "medication pill card". This can be done when a patient has a complicated drug regimen and/or lives in a long-term care facility. Repackaging a patient's drugs into a bubble pack would increase compliance and reduce medication errors.

Any pharmacy providing repackaging services must have P&Ps for the repackaging process, and must label the repackaged drugs with the following:

- All the information required for a prescription label.[105]

- The name and address of the pharmacy that initially dispensed the drugs to the patient, and the name and address of the pharmacy repackaging the drugs, if different.

---

104   B&PC 4052.7
105   B&PC 4076

## REFILL PHARMACIES

Retail pharmacies can use central fill (or refill) pharmacies to prepare new prescriptions and, more commonly, refills. If the two pharmacies use a common electronic file, P&Ps must be in place to prevent unauthorized disclosures. The originating pharmacy and the refill pharmacy must have a <u>contract</u> outlining the refill arrangement, or the pharmacies must have the <u>same owner</u>. In addition to the normal requirements for a container label, the name and address of the refilling and/or the originating pharmacy must be included on the label. The patient is provided with written information, either on the label or on the container that describes which pharmacy to contact for questions. Both pharmacies need to keep complete and accurate records of the refills, and both are responsible for the accuracy of the fills. The <u>originating</u> pharmacy is responsible for <u>counseling</u> patients, maintaining the <u>medication profiles</u> and performing a <u>drug utilization review</u> before delivery of each prescription.

## COMPOUNDING

The California compounding regulations closely mirrors the United States Pharmacopeia (USP) compounding standards. For more information, please see the following chapters in the RxPrep Course Book: Non-Sterile Compounding, Sterile Compounding, Handling Hazardous Drugs.

### Traditional Compounding and Section 503A

Sometimes, the health needs of a patient cannot be met by an FDA-approved medication and compounded drugs can fill the need. Compounding can be used for medically necessary reasons, such as changing the formulation to make it easier for the patient to take the drug, avoiding a non-essential ingredient to which the patient has an allergy or intolerance, or preparing a dose that is not commercially available. Traditional compounding is used for these purposes, and is defined under section 503A of the Drug Quality and Security Act (DQSA).

<u>Traditional compounding</u> is based on a prescription that has been written for an <u>individual patient</u>. Section 503A also permits pharmacists to prepare small batches of a compounded preparation in advance if the dispensing history of the pharmacy supports the need. The primary reason for this allowance is convenience: it takes time to set up ingredients and equipment, prepare the product, document the preparation, and clean the area. If a pharmacist in a medical building prepares 3 – 4 prescriptions of the same strength of a progesterone cream each day, the pharmacy can prepare a few days' worth of the cream so it is ready when the prescriptions are received. These preparations will need to be labeled with the appropriate beyond use date (BUD).

Pharmacies can sell compounded preparations to prescribers for <u>administration</u> or <u>application</u> to patients (human and animal) in the <u>prescriber's office</u>.[106] Prescribers <u>cannot</u> purchase compounded preparations from pharmacies to <u>furnish/dispense</u> to human patients. The prescriber's office will need to send a <u>purchase order</u> or other <u>documentation</u> to the pharmacy that <u>lists the patients</u> requiring the preparation. The <u>quantity</u> needed for each patient should be specified. The preparations are delivered to the prescriber's office and signed for by the prescriber or their agent.

106  CCR 1735.2(c)

Veterinarians can also purchase compounded preparations from a pharmacy for the purpose of <u>furnishing/dispensing</u> up to a <u>120-hour supply</u> of compounded preparations to their own <u>veterinary patients</u>.[107] This means a veterinarian can administer the compounded preparation to the veterinary patient in the office and/or give them a take-home supply. When veterinarians order compounded preparations from the pharmacy, the veterinarians must indicate how many veterinary patients they anticipate needing the compound for and must also indicate how much they anticipate using per veterinary patient (for office-use and for furnishing).

Traditional compounding includes any of the following:[108]

- <u>Altering</u> the <u>dosage form</u> or <u>delivery system</u>

- <u>Altering</u> the <u>strength</u>

- <u>Combining components</u> or <u>active ingredients</u>

- Preparing a drug product from <u>chemicals or bulk drug substances</u>

These activities are not defined as compounding:[109]

- <u>Reconstituting</u> a drug, according to the manufacturer's directions

- <u>Splitting</u> tablets

- Adding <u>flavoring</u> agents to an existing drug product in order to enhance palatability

Drugs made with traditional compounding methods have three <u>exemptions</u> from requirements that otherwise apply to prescription drugs:

- Complying with the FDA's current good manufacturing practices (CGMPs)

- Labeling with adequate directions for use

- The need to complete a New Drug Application (NDA) in order to have the end product FDA-approved

Pharmacies can also compound <u>patient-specific parenteral therapy</u> for other pharmacies.[110] One pharmacy may enter into a <u>contract</u> with another to compound a drug for parenteral therapy, where one pharmacy receives the prescription/order and dispenses the preparation but contracts with the another pharmacy to prepare the compound. Compounding can only begin after receiving a patient-specific prescription/order. The <u>label</u> on the dispensed compound must include the <u>name of both</u> the <u>compounding</u> pharmacy and the <u>dispensing</u> pharmacy.

107  CCR 1735.2(c)(3)
108  CCR 1735(a)
109  CCR 1735(b)
110  B&PC 4123

## Outsourcing Facilities and Section 503B

In 2012, a fungal meningitis outbreak due to contaminated methylprednisolone injections prepared at the infamous New England Compounding Center (NECC) led to over 700 fungal infections and 64 deaths nationwide.[111] NECC prepared vials of methylprednisolone injections in bulk in order to capitalize on a drug shortage and distributing the drug across state lines. The vials were contaminated due to unsanitary conditions and lack of aseptic technique. Pharmacists involved have been charged with murder, racketeering, and mail fraud due to the gross negligence involved with these preparations. This highly publicized public health crisis led to stricter compounding regulations nationwide.

Shortly after the NECC meningitis outbreak, the federal Food, Drug, and Cosmetic act was amended to add section 503B. This legislation permits specially licensed compounding facilities to operate as an "outsourcing facility" in order to prepare medications in bulk and without a prescription written for an individual patient as long as the facility met certain requirements. This is especially important in the event of drug shortages. To register as an outsourcing facility under 503B, the facility needs to be compounding sterile drugs for humans.

Facilities can operate as an outsourcing facility if the following requirements are met:

- The drugs must be compounded in compliance with current good manufacturing practices

- The facility is licensed as an outsourcing facility by the FDA and California Board of Pharmacy.[112] In addition, an outsourcing facility cannot be licensed as a sterile compounding pharmacy at the same time. An outsourcing facility cannot perform the functions of a pharmacy, such as filling individual prescriptions for individual patients.[113]

- The facility is subject to inspection by the FDA and California Board of Pharmacy.[114]

- The preparations must be made by or under the supervision of a licensed pharmacist.

- The facility must meet certain labeling requirements, drug reporting requirements, and adverse event reporting requirements.

111   https://www.cdc.gov/hai/outbreaks/meningitis.html (accessed 2018 Feb 16).
112   B&PC 4129
113   B&PC 4129(e)
114   B&PC 4129.1(c), B&PC 4129.2(c)

## Manufacturing vs Compounding

|  | MANUFACTURING | OUTSOURCING FACILITIES | TRADITIONAL COMPOUNDING |
|---|---|---|---|
| Regulated by | FDA | FDA, state board | State board |
| Standards/regulations | FDA drug approval process<br><br>Labeling with adequate directions for use<br><br>Current good manufacturing practices (CGMPs) | 503B<br><br>CGMPs<br><br>USP | 503A<br><br>USP |
| Individual prescription required | No | No | Yes |
| Interstate distribution | Yes | Yes | Up to 5% of total sales (the "5% rule") |

## Handling Hazardous Drugs

The National Institute for Occupational Safety and Health (NIOSH) issues a list of hazardous drugs (HDs) that require special precautions in order to prevent work-related injury and illness. HDs can cause harm to healthcare staff who handle them, including pharmacists, technicians, nurses and cleaning staff. Common HDs include antineoplastics (chemotherapy drugs), pregnancy category X drugs, hormones, and transplant drugs. The standard for handling drugs on the NIOSH list are set by the U.S. Pharmacopeia (USP), in Chapter 800. The California Board of Pharmacy has implemented regulations that closely mirror the USP 800 standards.[115]

Minimally, a pharmacy or other setting handling HDs must have the following:

- Engineering controls, such as closed system transfer devices and negative pressure ventilated cabinets (e.g., biological safety cabinets). The hoods vent the drug's toxic fumes to the outside (away from the staff standing at the hood).

- Personal protective equipment (e.g., chemotherapy gown, respiratory protection, goggles, two pairs of shoe covers, chemotherapy gloves). HDs will require either single or double gloves when handling.

- Safe work practices, spill kits, and disposal requirements.

For more information, refer to the RxPrep Course Book, Handling Hazardous Drugs chapter.

115   CCR Articles 4.5, 7 and 7.5

## NUCLEAR PHARMACY

Nuclear pharmacists compound and dispense radioactive drugs for diagnostic purposes or treatment. Due to the inherent danger of radioactive exposure and the need to reduce exposure with known techniques, pharmacists handling radioactive drugs must be competent in the preparation, storage and dispensing of radioactive drugs.[116] A pharmacist qualified in radioactive drug management must be in the pharmacy whenever radioactive drugs are being provided to medical staff. All personnel involved in the furnishing of radioactive drugs are under the immediate and direct supervision of a qualified nuclear pharmacist. Pharmacies that compound nuclear drugs must have a sterile compounding permit from the board.

## HOSPITAL PHARMACY

### Medication/Chart Order

Hospital medication orders, or chart orders, serve a similar purpose as prescriptions: they are the prescriber's orders for drugs and other items (such as labs and procedures) for their patients. An order would include similar information as a prescription, such as the patient's name, drug name, dose, frequency, and prescriber's signature. A prescriber can handwrite an order in the patient's physical paper chart or enter it into the patient's electronic medical record.

Prescribers can also issue face-to-face verbal and telephone orders for hospital patients. Written orders are preferred over verbal orders to reduce medication errors. However, prescribers may prefer to give a verbal order when they are too busy or may be off-site without access to the computerized provider order entry (CPOE) system or patient chart. There could be an emergency situation, such as a code, where a drug must be administered immediately. In this situation, it would be appropriate for a prescriber to issue a verbal order and authenticate it at a later time. For example, a nurse could report that a patient is experiencing nausea, and the prescriber could instruct the nurse to administer ondansetron. The nurse would enter the order, note the prescriber's name, and sign the order. The prescriber has 48 hours to physically or electronically countersign the order.[117]

A copy of the chart order for non-controlled substances must be kept at the hospital for at least three years.[118] All orders for controlled substances in a hospital setting must be kept for a minimum of seven years.[119]

In addition to individual medication orders, drugs can be provided under a standing order or protocol or order set, which are treatment plans designed to help direct acceptable care for select conditions. The use of standing orders, order sets and protocols will be described in the facility's P&Ps.

116   CCR 1708.4
117   22 CCR 70263(g)
118   B&PC 4081, B&PC 4105, B&PC 4333
119   H&SC 11159

## Centralized Hospital Packaging

The board has created a type of specialty license for a hospital pharmacy to perform centralized packaging for the pharmacy's hospital <u>and one or more general acute care hospitals</u> under <u>common ownership</u> and located <u>within a 75-mile radius</u> of each other. The centralized pharmacy can prepare and store a limited quantity of unit dose drugs in advance of a patient-specific prescription in amounts necessary to ensure continuity of care.

Drugs packaged as single units or "unit doses" are convenient for hospitals because it reduces drug diversion, drug waste, and medication errors. The unit dose container is a non-reusable container designed to hold a quantity of drug intended for direct, oral administration as a single dose. Unit dose packaging can be performed by the drug company or prepared from multiple dose containers in the pharmacy. Pharmacies repackage drugs from multiple dose containers into unit dose packaging on a routine basis.

<u>Barcoding</u> is essential for hospital safety since it will help verify that the right drug is given to the right patient. The nurse administering the drug will scan the barcode on the unit dose medication and then scan the barcode on the patient's wristband to make sure that it is the right medication, for the right inpatient, in the right dose, and via the right route of administration. Any unit dose medication produced by a centralized hospital packaging pharmacy must be barcoded to be <u>machine readable</u> at the <u>inpatient's bedside</u> using barcode medication administration software. The software must read the barcode and compare the information retrieved to the electronic medical record of the inpatient.[120]

The label for each unit dose medication produced by a centralized hospital packaging pharmacy must contain all of the following:[121]

- The date that the medication was prepared

- The beyond use date

- The name of the drug

- The quantity of each active ingredient

- Special storage or handling requirements

- The lot/control number assigned by the centralized hospital packaging pharmacy (a pharmacist must be able to retrieve the following information with the lot/control number: the components used in the drug, expiration date of each drug components, and NDC number)

- The name of the centralized hospital packaging pharmacy

---

120   B&PC 4128.4
121   B&PC 4128.5

According to United States Pharmacopeia (USP) guidelines, the beyond use date for unit dose containers is no later than either of the following:

- One year from the date the drug is repackaged

- Expiration date on manufacturer's container

### Drug Supply at Nursing Stations

Supplies of drugs for use in medical emergencies must be immediately available at each nursing unit or service area.[122] The emergency drug supply must be stored in a clearly marked portable container which is sealed by the pharmacist in such a manner that a seal must be broken to gain access to the drugs. The contents of the container must be listed on the outside cover and must include the earliest expiration date of any drugs within.

### Monthly Inspection of Drug Supply

The hospital drug supply must be inspected by a pharmacist, intern, or technician at least every 30 days.[123] This includes automated dispensing machines, refrigerator, freezer, emergency supply stock. The inspection should include removing outdated, unusable (adulterated), recalled, and mislabeled (misbranded) drugs. Look-alike, sound-alike drugs should not be stored close to each other. Records of inspections must be kept for at least three years. Irregularities must be reported within 24 hours to the pharmacist in charge and the director or chief executive officer of the healthcare facility.

### INTERNET PHARMACIES

There are generally two types of Internet pharmacies: legitimate mail order pharmacies and rogue Internet pharmacies. Legitimate mail order pharmacies dispense medications to patients (human or animal) only with a prescription from a prescriber who has performed an appropriate exam, while rogue pharmacies do not.[124]

Rogue pharmacies are used by those who do not have a valid prescription for a drug they desire, or by patients seeking lower-priced drugs. The drugs purchased from rogue pharmacies have a high probability of being counterfeit. The National Association of Boards of Pharmacy (NABP) reviewed 11,000 online pharmacies and found that 96% do not meet safe, legal requirements. This information is available on www.AWARErx.org.[125]

In 2008, the federal Ryan Haight Online Pharmacy Consumer Protection Act was signed into law to regulate Internet pharmacies that sell controlled substances. In order to legally dispense controlled substances through an online pharmacy, the pharmacy must register with the DEA and report their dispensing activity to the DEA.

---

122   22 CCR 70263(f)
123   22 CCR 70263(f), B&PC 4119.7(c), B&PC 4115(i)(3)
124   B&PC 4067(a)
125   http://www.pharmacy.ca.gov/consumers/parents_internet_pharmacies.pdf (accessed 2018 Feb 16).

## DISPENSING EPINEPHRINE AUTO INJECTORS

A pharmacist can dispense epinephrine auto-injectors (*EpiPen*) to a pre-hospital emergency medical care person, lay rescuer, or authorized entity for first aid purposes.[126, 127] The responder has to obtain current certification demonstrating that the person is trained and qualified to administer the auto-injector.

A physician provides a written order that specifies the quantity of epinephrine auto-injectors to be dispensed. Each epinephrine auto-injector should be dispensed with the manufacturer's product information sheet, and labelled with the following:

■ The name of the person to whom the prescription was issued

■ The designation "Section 1797.197a responder" and "First Aid Purposes Only"

■ The dosage, use, and expiration date

A pharmacy can also provide auto-injectors for a school district or charter school, based on a physician/surgeon written order.[128]

If someone gives an epinephrine injection in good faith to try and help someone who is having anaphylaxis, they are given immunity from prosecution and no civil damages can be awarded.

## DISPENSING BLOOD CLOTTING PRODUCTS FOR HOME USE

Hemophilia and Von Willebrand disease are hereditary bleeding disorders. Until the 1970s, people with severe hemophilia suffered from uncontrollable internal bleeding, orthopedic deformities, and a shortened lifespan. More recently, the production of highly purified blood clotting factors has provided people with bleeding disorders the opportunity to lead normal lives. The preferred method of treatment of hemophilia today is intravenous injection, or infusion, of prescription blood clotting products at a federally designated regional hemophilia treatment center. Pharmacies and other entities specializing in the delivery of blood clotting products and related equipment, supplies, and services for home use form a growing enterprise in California. Timely access to federally designated regional hemophilia centers and appropriate products/services in the home reduces mortality and bleeding-related hospitalizations.

Each provider of blood clotting products for home use must:[129]

■ Maintain 24-hour on-call service seven days a week for every day of the year, screen telephone calls for emergencies, acknowledge all telephone calls within one hour, and have access to knowledgeable pharmacy staffing on call 24 hours a day, to initiate emergency requests for clotting factors.

126   B&PC 4119.3
127   B&PC 4119.4
128   B&PC 4119.2
129   H&SC 125286.25

- Have the ability to obtain <u>all FDA-approved blood clotting products</u> in multiple assay ranges (low, medium, and high, as applicable) and vial sizes.

- Supply all necessary ancillary <u>infusion equipment and supplies</u> with each prescription, as needed.

- Ship the prescribed blood clotting products and ancillary infusion equipment and supplies to the patient within <u>two business days</u>.

## DISPENSING DRUGS DURING A FEDERAL, STATE, OR LOCAL EMERGENCY

Pharmacy law requirements can be waived during declared disasters and emergencies to ensure that patients receive medications. A pharmacist can dispense drugs (controlled and non-controlled) and devices in reasonable quantities without a prescription during a federal, state, or local emergency.[130] A record containing the <u>date, patient's name, and patient's address, and the name, strength, and quantity of the dispensed drug or device</u> must be maintained. The pharmacist must make a good faith effort to communicate this information to the patient's healthcare provider as soon as possible.

During a declared federal, state, or local emergency, the board can allow the deployment of a <u>mobile pharmacy</u> in impacted areas in order to ensure the continuity of patient care, if all of the following conditions are met:

- The mobile pharmacy shares common ownership with at least one currently licensed pharmacy in good standing.

- The mobile pharmacy retains records of dispensing.

- A licensed pharmacist is on-site and managing the mobile pharmacy.

- Reasonable security measures are taken to safeguard the drug supply maintained in the mobile pharmacy.

- The mobile pharmacy is located within the declared emergency area or affected areas.

- The mobile pharmacy ceases activity within <u>48 hours</u> after the emergency is over.

A recent example of this was in December 2017, when the president and the state governor declared a state of emergency due to the wildfires in Southern California. Due to this emergency, the board allows pharmacies in the affected areas to furnish residents with medically necessary drugs for themselves and their pets, without presentation of a prescription or drug container, even if prescriptions are not on file with the pharmacy.

130   B&PC 4062

## REFUSAL TO DISPENSE BASED ON RELIGIOUS, MORAL, OR ETHICAL BELIEFS

The pharmacist's right to refuse dispensing certain medications (e.g., emergency contraception, oral contraceptives, abortion pills, erectile dysfunction drugs, and aid-in-dying drugs) based on religious or moral grounds has been a controversial issue in the United States.

In California, a pharmacist can refuse to dispense certain medications if he or she has previously notified his or her employer, in writing, and written protocols are established to ensure that the patient has timely access to the prescribed drug or device despite the pharmacist's refusal to dispense the prescription or order. This can mean having another staff pharmacist dispensing the drug or referring the patient to a nearby pharmacy.[131]

## TEST ORDERING, INTERPRETATION, AND MANAGEMENT

The California Pharmacist Association has developed guidelines for pharmacists ordering and managing tests to ensure safe and appropriate medication therapy.[132] The key principles are reviewed below:

- Testing should be for ensuring safe and effective medication therapy in coordination with the patient's PCP or with the diagnosing prescriber

- Tests must only be ordered when necessary

- Test results must be managed appropriately and promptly, and patients should receive feedback on their tests in a timely manner

- Quality assurance should be integrated into the test ordering, interpretation, and the management process

Pharmacists are individually responsible for personal competence in ordering tests and interpreting results. Variables that may impact test results must be considered by pharmacists when interpreting results including timing of testing, medications, renal or hepatic function, fluid status, lab error, etc. Here are examples where ordering lab results would be appropriate: serum drug levels for medications with narrow therapeutic indexes (e.g., lithium, antipsychotics, anticonvulsants), INR for warfarin patients, renal and hepatic function tests for medications requiring dose adjustment in renal or hepatic impairment, culture and sensitivity results for antibiotic therapy and selection of appropriate drug therapy.

Pharmacists who order tests should be available, or have back-up available, to respond in a timely manner to critical results. At a minimum, a pharmacist should relay the critical value to the provider with primary responsibility for that aspect of the patient's care. Critical values must be reported in the time frame indicated in the protocol for management of the condition, if present. If a test result does not appear reasonable, it should be repeated. Pharmacists should refer patients to other healthcare professionals as problems are identified that require additional care.

131  B&PC 733(b)(3)
132  https://cpha.com/wp-content/uploads/2017/09/Guidelines-for-pharmacists-ordering-tests-in-California-5-0.pdf (accessed 2018 Feb 16).

All actions related to test ordering, interpretation, and management, including changes in drug treatment, must be documented within 24 hours in a system accessible to the healthcare team members. Preferably, the electronic health record (EHR) should be available in the pharmacist's work settings. A large benefit with the use of EHRs is a reduction in unnecessary or duplicative testing.

Pharmacists should include each of the following items when they document changes in care:

■ Interpretation of the result

■ Rationale for the decision

■ Information provided to the patient and the healthcare team members

A quality assurance (QA) assessment should be used to document the quality of the pharmacist's care.

## FURNISHING AND ADMINISTERING DRUGS & DEVICES

### Administering Injectable Drugs and Biologics

Prior to SB 493, all pharmacists could administer only oral and topical drugs that had been ordered by a prescriber, and pharmacists who were trained in immunizations could administer vaccines. Now, all licensed pharmacists can administer drugs and biologics by other routes, including by injection. Most pharmacists are trained in administering vaccines. However, not all injectable drugs are administered the same way vaccines are. If a pharmacist will be administering injectable drugs and biologics as part of their practice, the pharmacist should receive adequate training.

Intramuscular (IM) injection generally hurts more than receiving a subcutaneous (SC) injection due to the longer needle length and subsequent muscle soreness, but can end up being better tolerated if the drug itself is irritating to SC tissue. In adults, intramuscular (IM) injections are given in the deltoid muscle at the central and thickest portion above the level of the armpit and below the acromion. Emerging evidence suggests providers may be giving IM vaccines too high on the deltoid; make sure to give in the thickest, most central part of the deltoid. Adults require a 1" needle (or a 1½" needle for women greater than 200 lbs or men greater than 260 pounds). Use a 22-25 gauge needle inserted at a 90 degree angle. The higher the gauge, the thinner the needle. Subcutaneous (SC) vaccinations are given in the fatty tissue over the triceps with a 5/8", 23-25 gauge needle at a 45 degree angle.

Multiple injections given in the same extremity should be separated by a minimum of 1 inch, if possible. For patients that require frequent injections, SC and IM injection sites are rotated to avoid irritation. In most cases, the concurrent use of injectable vasoconstrictors is not recommended due to the risk of abscess, except when localized drug administration is desired, such as the use of epinephrine and lidocaine for anesthesia within a localized area.

Some injectable drugs can be absorbed faster with heat or massage (for example, the *EpiPen* instructions state to massage the area for 10 seconds after injecting). With drugs that can cause easy bruising (such as anticoagulants), it is important not to massage the area.

With all injections, there must be an emergency protocol to treat severe reactions as described in the RxPrep Course Book Immunizations chapter. The pharmacy will need to have an additional protocol for needle-stick injuries. Safe syringe disposal must be practiced, which is discussed in the Medication Safety & Quality Improvement chapter.[133]

## Initiating and Administering Immunizations

Pharmacists in California can independently administer <u>routine</u> immunizations to adults and children ages <u>3 years</u> and older.[134] The routine immunizations are those recommended by the Advisory Committee on Immunization Practices (ACIP), and published by the Centers for Disease Control and Prevention (CDC). A physician-directed protocol may be used if administering non-routine immunizations. A pharmacist can also initiate and administer <u>epinephrine</u> or <u>diphenhydramine</u> by injection to treat a severe allergic reaction.

Pharmacists and interns who initiate and administer vaccines must:

- Complete a CDC or ACIP-approved <u>immunization training program</u>.

- Maintain <u>basic life support certification</u>.

- Complete <u>one hour</u> of continuing education on immunizations and vaccines every <u>two years</u>.

In order for intern pharmacists to administer vaccines, <u>both</u> the supervising pharmacist and the intern must have completed an approved immunization training program. This is true for other activities that require special training or certification; if the pharmacist is not trained or certified in the activity, they will not be able to adequately supervise interns performing the activity.

The pharmacist must also comply with the following recordkeeping and reporting requirements:

- Pharmacist must notify each patient's <u>primary care provider</u> (PCP) and each pregnant patient's <u>prenatal care provider</u> (if applicable) within <u>14 days</u> of the administration of any vaccine. If the patient does not have a PCP, the pharmacist should advise the patient to consult with a healthcare provider of their choice.

---

133   *http://www.immunize.org/catg.d/p2020.pdf (accessed 2018 Feb 16).*
134   *B&PC 4052(a)(11)*

- Pharmacists must report the administration of any vaccine to the <u>California Immunization Registry</u> (CAIR). Pharmacies (not pharmacists) must be enrolled in CAIR. It is optional for individual pharmacists to enroll in CAIR.

- A <u>patient vaccine administration record</u> must be kept and readily retrievable during the pharmacy's normal business hours. A pharmacist must provide each patient with a vaccine administration record.

Effective January, 2016, all children (kindergarten to 12th grade) in public or private schools (i.e., not home-schooled) have to be immunized prior to admittance. Medical exemptions may be permitted, but personal belief exemptions have been eliminated.[135] Schools should be able to review the vaccination history on the immunization registry.

## Furnishing Emergency Contraception

The two types of medications approved for emergency contraception (EC) are <u>levonorgestrel</u> and <u>ulipristal</u>. Alternatively, a pharmacist can furnish <u>high-dose birth control pills</u> off-label to be used as EC.[136] *Plan B One-Step* and the generic formulations contain a single dose of 1.5 mg levonorgestrel. *Plan B* and the generic formulations contain two tablets; each contains half the dose of levonorgestrel (0.75 mg). The two-tablet formulation was the first type of levonorgestrel approved for use as EC. Since that time, the FDA concluded that there is no clear advantage of the two-tablet over the one-tablet formulation. Ulipristal (*Ella*) is a single dose, 1-tablet EC product available only by <u>prescription</u>. Levonorgestrel and ulipristal have similar efficacy during the first <u>72 hours</u> (3 days) after unprotected intercourse. Levonorgestrel and ulipristal can both be recommended for up to <u>120 hours</u> (5 days), but ulipristal is more effective from 72 – 120 hours (3 – 5 days) after unprotected intercourse. EC has not been shown to cause harm to a developing fetus, and does not impair a woman's ability to conceive in the future. If the woman has taken EC and does not have a menstrual period within 3 weeks, she should get a pregnancy test.

EC can be obtained by three options:

1. OTC

2. Prescription

3. Furnished by a pharmacist in California under the board's EC protocol

---

135   *SB 277*
136   *http://ec.princeton.edu/get-EC-now.html (accessed 2018 Feb 16).*

### EC: OTC Option

*Plan B One-Step* and similar products can be purchased <u>OTC, without sex, age or identification requirements</u>. Some of the generic formulations state that the product is intended for women ages 17 years and older, however, this is not a sale restriction. EC can be purchased at anytime the store is open, including times when the pharmacy section is closed. The FDA has requested that the OTC EC products be kept in the aisle with other family planning items, such as condoms and spermicide. For the <u>two-tablet levonorgestrel products</u>, there are still <u>age restrictions</u> and these must be kept <u>behind the pharmacy counter</u>. A pharmacy staff member must check ID to ensure the person purchasing the product is age <u>17 or older</u>.

### EC: Prescription Option

A prescription for EC can be given to the pharmacist that was issued from an outside prescriber. If a <u>prescription is received</u>, the pharmacist <u>dispenses</u> the EC as they would other prescription drugs. The OTC cost for EC is \$35 – \$50, and some women will prefer to use insurance coverage if the prescription copay is lower than the OTC cost. The Affordable Care Act (ACA, or Obamacare) requires coverage for "essential health services", described further. This includes "women's preventive services", including contraception and EC, at no cost-sharing for the patient. Under the ACA, EC is covered only with a <u>prescription</u> written for a <u>female</u> patient.[137,138] The only insurance plans under the ACA (which can be found in the health insurance marketplace called "*Covered California*") that may not cover EC are grandfathered health plans (which have been permitted to retain some of their original features for a set time period) or religiously-exempt employer health plans.

### EC: Procotol Option

A pharmacist can <u>furnish</u> EC under the board's protocol.[139] A patient might choose this option if she does <u>not have a prescription</u> from a prescriber and <u>wishes to use insurance coverage</u>. In order to furnish EC under the protocol, the pharmacist must have completed one hour of CE on emergency contraception. The pharmacist must ask and communicate the following to the patient:

■ Are you <u>allergic</u> to any medications?

■ Timing is an essential element of the product's effectiveness. Emergency contraception should be taken as soon as possible after unprotected intercourse. Treatment can begin up to <u>five days (120 hours)</u> after unprotected intercourse.

■ Emergency contraception use <u>will not interfere with an established or implanted pregnancy</u>.

137   https://www.gpo.gov/fdsys/pkg/FR-2013-07-02/pdf/2013-15866.pdf (accessed 2018 Feb 16).
138   http://www.hrsa.gov/womensguidelines/ (accessed 2018 Feb 16).
139   CCR 1746

■ If more than 72 hours have elapsed since the unprotected intercourse, the use of *Ella* may be preferred. For other options for emergency contraception, consult with your healthcare provider.[140]

■ Please follow up with your healthcare provider after the use of emergency contraception.

EC can be furnished for <u>future use</u>. This means that a patient can pick up a box of EC to keep at home in the event that unprotected intercourse recurs. There are no product quantity limits.

An EC Fact Sheet (shown on the next page) must be provided to the patient when furnishing emergency contraception.[141] The board's website provides the Fact Sheet in 10 languages. The pharmacist should answer any questions the patient may have, and record the necessary information into the patient's medication record as required for any prescription. Recall that if a pharmacist has a reasonable belief that the patient will not continue to obtain prescriptions from that pharmacy, such as an out-of-town patient who is visiting the area, a medication profile will not be required.[142]

The pharmacy should maintain an inventory of EC medications and adjunctive medications indicated for nausea and vomiting (N/V). There is a higher incidence of N/V with estrogen-containing EC, compared to levonorgestrel (progestin-only) formulations. Patients will need to be given information concerning dosing and potential adverse effects.

A pharmacist can provide up to 12 non-spermicidal condoms to each Medi-Cal and Family Planning, Access, Care, and Treatment (PACT) client who obtains EC. Medi-Cal and Family PACT are programs for low-income residents of California. Family PACT focuses on family planning, and provides contraception coverage.

If a pharmacist refuses to dispense EC, the pharmacy must have a protocol in place to ensure that the patient has timely access to the drug.[143] If EC is not immediately available at the pharmacy (e.g., if it is out of stock or if the only pharmacist on duty refuses to dispense it), the pharmacist will need to refer the patient to another EC provider.

---

140    *A copper intrauterine device (IUD) can be inserted within five days of unprotected intercourse, and will provide the benefit of ongoing contraception.*

141    *http://www.pharmacy.ca.gov/publications/emer_contraception.pdf (accessed 2018 Feb 16).*

142    *CCR 1707.1(a)*

143    *CCR 1746(b)(5), B&PC 733(b)(3)*

# Key Facts About Emergency Contraception

Emergency Contraception (EC) is a safe and effective way to prevent pregnancy after sex.

Consider using Emergency Contraception (EC) if:
- You had unprotected sex, or
- You think your contraceptive didn't work.

What are Emergency Contraceptive pills?
Emergency Contraceptive pills contain the same medication as regular birth control pills, and help to prevent pregnancy. There are three basic types of Emergency Contraceptive pills:

- Progestin-only pills (Plan B® One-Step, Next Choice®)
- Ulipristate acetate (ella®)
- High doses of regular oral contraceptive pills

Don't wait! Take EC as soon as possible.
- It is best to take EC as soon as possible; the sooner you take EC the more effective it is.
- It has been shown to be effective for up to 5 days.
- For more information talk to your pharmacist or doctor.

When taken as directed Emergency Contraception has been shown to be safe and effective.
- Emergency Contraception may reduce the risk of pregnancy by up to 89 percent.
- The effectiveness of EC varies based on the type used and when it is taken.
- EC is only recommended as a backup and should not be used as your primary method of birth control.
- Emergency Contraceptive pills do not protect against sexually transmitted infections, including HIV/AIDS.

What EC does:
- Emergency Contraceptive pills prevent pregnancy.
- Emergency Contraceptive pills are not effective after pregnancy has occurred and they will not harm the developing fetus.
- Emergency Contraceptive pills are NOT the same as RU-486 (the abortion pill).
- Using Emergency Contraceptive pills will not affect a woman's ability to become pregnancy in the future.

Follow-up after taking Emergency Contraceptive pills:
- If you vomit after taking emergency contraception you may need to take another dose. Before you do, contact a pharmacist or healthcare provider immediately.
- If you do not get a normal period within three weeks, take a pregnancy test.
- It is important to visit your doctor or clinic for a regular birth control method and information about preventing sexually transmitted infections.
- Medical providers or your pharmacist can provide Emergency Contraception for future use if needed.

In California, women and men may receive free family planning services through Family PACT based on income.

If you don't have a doctor or clinic, call (800) 942-1054 to find a Family PACT provider near you.

Under the Affordable Care Act (ACA), Emergency Contraception may be covered with a prescription.

 **BE AWARE AND TAKE CARE:**
Talk to your pharmacist!
CALIFORNIA STATE BOARD OF PHARMACY

California State Board of Pharmacy
1625 North Market Blvd., Suite N-219
Sacramento, CA 95834

www.pharmacy.ca.gov
(916) 574-7900

*Image courtesy of the California Board of Pharmacy*

## Furnishing Naloxone

The rising death toll due to inappropriate/excessive opioid use has spurred a national movement to make naloxone more widely available to the public. Naloxone is an <u>opioid antagonist</u> that binds to and displaces the opioid from the receptor sites. Naloxone reverses the action of the opioid, including <u>overdose</u> symptoms and analgesia; in chronic users, the abrupt reversal with naloxone will cause <u>opioid withdrawal</u> symptoms, which can be severe.

The new auto-injector *Evzio* has visual and voice instructions that make administration quite simple, although the protocol covers the use of <u>all FDA-approved naloxone formulations</u>, including the injection (generic naloxone) and the nasal spray (*Narcan*).

Naloxone can be given if opioid overdose is <u>suspected</u> due to respiratory symptoms and/or symptoms of CNS depression. Similar to epinephrine, if there is a question about whether the drug should be used, use it, since fatality could result from lack of use.

Emergency care will be required and anyone administering naloxone must call 911. Symptoms of opioid overdose (from legal or illicit use) include:

- Extreme or unusual somnolence (cannot be awakened verbally or with a firm sternal rub)

- Respiratory difficulty, ranging from slow or shallow breathing to complete respiratory arrest

- Miosis (very small "pinpoint" pupils)

- Bradycardia

**Pharmacists Furnishing Naloxone Pursuant to Board Protocol**

Pharmacists furnishing naloxone according to the board protocol must follow these steps[144,145]:

- Complete <u>one hour</u> of CE on the use of naloxone, or an equivalent curriculum-based training program from a board-recognized school of pharmacy.

- Ask if the recipient uses opioids or knows someone who does.

- Ask if the recipient has a known naloxone hypersensitivity.

- Provide the recipient with training in opioid overdose prevention, recognition, response and on the administration of naloxone. When dispensing naloxone, <u>patient counseling cannot be waived</u>.

- Provide the board-approved Fact Sheet. With the patient's permission, the pharmacist must notify the patient's PCP that naloxone was furnished.

- Keep records of furnishing the naloxone for 3 years.

**Pharmacies Furnishing Naloxone to Schools Pursuant to a Prescription**

Pharmacies can furnish naloxone to a <u>school district</u>, <u>county office of education</u>, or <u>charter school</u> pursuant to a prescriber's <u>prescription</u>.[146, 147] School nurses and trained volunteers use the naloxone to treat opioid overdose.

144  http://www.pharmacy.ca.gov/publications/naloxone_protocol.pdf (accessed 2018 Feb 16).
145  http://www.pharmacy.ca.gov/publications/naloxone_fact_sheet.pdf (accessed 2018 Feb 16).
146  B&PC 4119.8
147  Education Code 49414.3

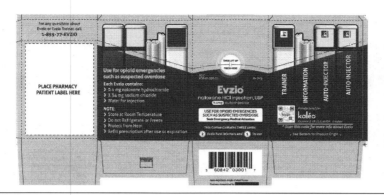

The *Evzio* package includes a trainer & 2 auto-injectors. The injector is nearly identical to the *Auvi-Q* epinephrine auto-injector. Both *Evzio* and *Auvi-Q* have a safety cover that is removed. They are injected straight into the outer thigh by pressing the device against the skin or given through clothing. Both cause a hiss-and-click sound when the injection is given, and are held against the thigh for 5 seconds to allow time for the drug to disperse.

## How to give naloxone:

There are 3 ways to give naloxone. Follow the instructions for the type you have.

### Nasal spray naloxone

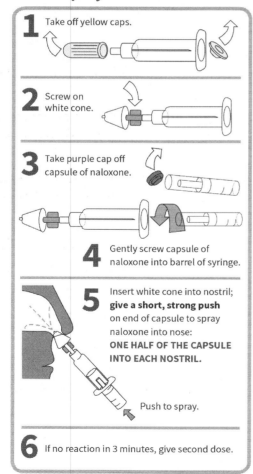

**1** Take off yellow caps.

**2** Screw on white cone.

**3** Take purple cap off capsule of naloxone.

**4** Gently screw capsule of naloxone into barrel of syringe.

**5** Insert white cone into nostril; **give a short, strong push** on end of capsule to spray naloxone into nose: **ONE HALF OF THE CAPSULE INTO EACH NOSTRIL.**

Push to spray.

**6** If no reaction in 3 minutes, give second dose.

### Injectable naloxone

**1** Remove cap from naloxone vial and uncover the needle.

**2** Insert needle through rubber plug with vial upside down. Pull back on plunger and take up 1 ml.

fill to 1 ml

**3** Inject 1 ml of naloxone into an upper arm or thigh muscle.

**4** If no reaction in 3 minutes, give second dose.

### Auto-injector

The naloxone auto-injector is FDA approved for use by anyone in the community. It contains a speaker that provides instructions to inject naloxone into the outer thigh, through clothing if needed.

Image courtesy of the California Board of Pharmacy

## Furnishing Prescription Nicotine Replacement Therapy

Tobacco dependence is a chronic illness that typically requires repeated interventions and multiple attempts to quit. Effective treatments exist that can significantly increase rates of long-term abstinence.[148]

As part of their normal practice, pharmacists recommend OTC products, including the nicotine patch and gum. Under the protocol, pharmacists can furnish prescription NRT (including the inhaler and nasal spray) by following these steps[149]:

- Completes a minimum of two hours of an approved CE program specific to smoking cessation therapy and NRT, or an equivalent curriculum-based training program completed within the last two years at an accredited California school of pharmacy.

- Completes ongoing CE focused on smoking cessation therapy every two years.

- Reviews the patient's current tobacco use and past quit attempts.

- Asks the patient a series of screening questions:

  - Are you pregnant or plan to become pregnant? (If yes, do not furnish and refer to an appropriate healthcare provider.)

  - Have you had a heart attack within the last 2 weeks? (If yes, furnish with caution and refer to an appropriate healthcare provider.)

  - Do you have any history of heart palpitations, irregular heartbeats, or have you been diagnosed with a serious arrhythmia? (If yes, furnish with caution and refer to an appropriate healthcare provider.)

  - Do you currently experience frequent chest pain or have you been diagnosed with unstable angina? (If yes, furnish with caution and refer to an appropriate healthcare provider.)

  - Do you have any history of allergic rhinitis (e.g., nasal allergies)? (If yes, avoid nasal spray.)

  - Have you been diagnosed with temporal mandibular joint (TMJ) dysfunction? (If yes, avoid nicotine gum.)

- Counsels patients on therapy and refers for further smoking cessation support.

- Notifies the patient's PCP of the drugs or devices provided or enters the information in a shared patient record system. If the patient does not have a PCP, the pharmacist provides the patient with a written record of what they received, and advises the patient to consult a PCP of their choice.

- The records of furnishing the NRT are kept for three years.

---

148   Review the RxPrep Course Book Tobacco Cessation chapter.
149   CCR 1746.2

## Furnishing Self-Administered Hormonal Contraceptives

A pharmacist can furnish <u>self-administered hormonal contraceptives</u>, which includes oral formulations (birth control <u>pills</u>), transdermal (the <u>patch</u>, such as *Xulane*), vaginal (the <u>ring</u>, such as *NuvaRing*) and <u>injection</u> (such as *Depo-SubQ Provera*).[150]

Pharmacists who participate in this protocol must have complete at least <u>one hour</u> of a board-approved continuing education program specific to self-administered hormonal contraception, application of the <u>United States Medical Eligibility Criteria (USMEC)</u> for contraceptive use, and other CDC guidance on contraception. An equivalent, curriculum-based training program completed on or after the year 2014 in an accredited California school of pharmacy is also sufficient training to participate in this protocol.

The protocol requires that the pharmacist complete these steps:

- Ask the patient to complete the <u>self-screening form</u>; the form is based on the current US-MEC, developed by the CDC. The patient will need to complete the self-screening form <u>initially</u> and again <u>annually</u>, or whenever the patient indicates a <u>major health change</u>. The pharmacist reviews the answers and clarifies responses; the use of contraception <u>may be prohibited based on the responses</u>, such as having a history of breast cancer, heart disease, DVT, or tobacco use. The form includes questions that can identify the use of drugs that could decrease the contraceptive efficacy, such as drugs for epilepsy which are enzyme inducers. If the pharmacist finds that it is not safe to provide the contraception or that the efficacy could be impaired, the patient should be referred to their PCP or to a nearby clinic for further assistance. The self-screening form should be available in languages commonly seen at the pharmacy.

---

150   CCR 1746.1, B&PC 4052.3

- Measure and record the patient's seated <u>blood pressure</u> if <u>combined (estrogen and progestin) hormonal contraceptives</u> are requested or recommended.

- Ensure that the patient is trained in administration and has received counseling on the product, including: (1) the dose, (2) the effectiveness, (3) potential side effects, (4) safety concerns, (5) the importance of receiving preventative health screenings, and (6) the lack of protection against sexually transmitted infections. The medication dispensed will be documented in the patient's profile.

- Provide the patient with three fact sheets: (1) a birth control guide such as the one from the FDA (see following page)[151], (2) the <u>patient product information</u> (PPI), and (3) an administration fact sheet for the specific formulation.

- Refer all patients to their PCP or to a nearby clinic for follow-up. Notify the patient's PCP of any drugs or devices furnished. If the patient does not have a PCP, the pharmacist must provide the patient with a written record of drugs/devices provided.

- If self-administered hormonal contraception services are not immediately available or the pharmacist declines to provide them based on a conscience clause, the pharmacist must refer the patient to another pharmacist or facility to get the product the patient has requested. State mandatory reporting laws (discussed further) must be followed if sexual abuse is suspected.

- Keep the records for three years.

---

151   https://www.fda.gov/downloads/ForConsumers/ByAudience/ForWomen/FreePublications/UCM517406.pdf (accessed 2018 Feb 16).

## BIRTH CONTROL GUIDE

**FDA U.S. FOOD & DRUG ADMINISTRATION**
www.fda.gov/birthcontrol

If you do not want to get pregnant, there are many birth control options to choose from. No one product is best for everyone. Some methods are more effective than others at preventing pregnancy. Check the pregnancy rates on this chart to get an idea of how effective the product is at preventing pregnancy. The pregnancy rates tell you the number of pregnancies expected per 100 women during the first year of typical use. Typical use shows how effective the different methods are during actual use (including sometimes using a method in a way that is not correct or not consistent). The only sure way to avoid pregnancy is not to have any sexual contact. Talk to your healthcare provider about the best method for you.

| FDA-Approved Methods | Number of pregnancies expected (per 100 Women)* | Use | Some Risks or Side Effects* This chart does not list all of the risks and side effects for each product. |
|---|---|---|---|
| Sterilization Surgery for Women | Less than 1 | Onetime procedure. Permanent. | Pain / Bleeding / Infection or other complications after surgery |
| Sterilization Implant for Women | Less than 1 | Onetime procedure. Permanent. | Pain/ cramping / Pelvic or back discomfort / Vaginal bleeding |
| Sterilization Surgery for Men | Less than 1 | Onetime procedure. Permanent. | Pain / Bleeding / Infection |
| IUD Copper | Less than 1 | Inserted by a healthcare provider. Lasts up to 10 years. | Cramps / Heavier, longer periods / Spotting between periods |
| IUD with Progestin | Less than 1 | Inserted by a healthcare provider. Lasts up to 3-5 years, depending on the type. | Irregular bleeding / No periods (amenorrhea) / Abdominal/pelvic pain |
| Implantable Rod | Less than 1 | Inserted by a healthcare provider. Lasts up to 3 years. | Menstrual Changes / Weight gain / Acne / Mood swings or depressed mood / Headache |
| Shot/ Injection | 6 | Need a shot every 3 months. | Loss of bone density / Irregular bleeding/ Bleeding between periods / Headaches / Nervousness / Abdominal discomfort / Weight gain / Dizziness |
| Oral Contraceptives "The Pill" (Combined Pill) | 9 | Must swallow a pill every day. | Spotting/ bleeding between periods / Nausea / Breast tenderness / Headache |
| Oral Contraceptives "The Pill" (Extended/ Continuous Use Combined Pill) | 9 | Must swallow a pill every day. | Spotting/ bleeding between periods / Nausea / Breast tenderness / Headache |
| Oral Contraceptives "The Mini Pill" (Progestin Only) | 9 | Must swallow a pill at the same time every day. | Spotting/ bleeding between periods / Nausea / Breast tenderness / Headache |
| Patch | 9 | Put on a new patch each week for 3 weeks (21 total days). Don't put on a patch during the fourth week. | Spotting or bleeding between menstrual periods / Nausea / Breast tenderness / Skin irritation / Stomach pain / Headache |
| Vaginal Contraceptive Ring | 9 | Put the ring into the vagina yourself. Keep the ring in your vagina for 3 weeks and then take it out for one week. | Vaginal discharge, discomfort in the vagina, and mild irritation. / Headache / Nausea / Mood changes / Breast tenderness |
| Diaphragm with Spermicide | 12 | Must use every time you have sex. | Irritation / Allergic reactions / Urinary tract infection |
| Sponge with Spermicide | 12-24 | Must use every time you have sex. | Irritation |
| Cervical Cap with Spermicide | 17-23 | Must use every time you have sex. | Irritation / Allergic reactions / Abnormal Pap test |
| Male Condom | 18 | Must use every time you have sex. Provides protection against some STDs. | Irritation / Allergic reactions |
| Female Condom | 21 | Must use every time you have sex. Provides protection against some STDs. | Discomfort or pain during insertion or sex. / Burning sensation, rash or itching |
| Spermicide Alone | 28 | Must use every time you have sex. | Irritation / Allergic reactions / Urinary tract infection |

### OTHER CONTRACEPTION

**Emergency Contraceptives (EC):**

May be used if you did not use birth control or if your regular birth control fails (such as a condom breaks). It should not be used as a regular form of birth control. Emergency contraception prevents about 55 - 85% of predicted pregnancies.

| | | | |
|---|---|---|---|
| Levonorgestrel 1.5 mg (1 pill) Levonorgestrel .75 mg (2 pills) | 7 out of every 8 women who would have gotten pregnant will not become pregnant after taking this EC. | Swallow the pills as soon as possible within 3 days after having unprotected sex. | Menstrual changes / Headache / Dizziness / Breast pain / Lower stomach (abdominal) pain / Nausea / Vomiting / Tiredness |
| Ulipristal Acetate | 6 or 7 out of every 10 women who would have gotten pregnant will not become pregnant after taking this EC. | Swallow the pills within 5 days after having unprotected sex. | Headache / Abdominal pain / Tiredness / Nausea / Menstrual pain / Dizziness |

*For more information on the chance of getting pregnant while using a method or on the risks of a specific product, please check the product label or Trussell, J. (2011). "Contraceptive failure in the United States." Contraception 83(5).397-404.

*Most Effective* ↑ *Least Effective*

## Furnishing Travel Medications

A pharmacist can furnish travel medications under authority provided by SB 493 that do not require a diagnosis. This covers medications for travel <u>outside of the United States</u>. The prescription drug must be for either a condition that is both self-diagnosable and self-treatable according to the CDC, or for prophylaxis (for example, providing drugs for malaria prevention). [152,153]

In order to furnish travel medications, the pharmacist must meet the following requirements:

- Complete an approved <u>immunization certificate program</u>.

- Complete an approved <u>travel medicine training program</u>, which must consist of at least <u>10 hours</u> and cover each element of *The International Society of Travel Medicine's Body of Knowledge for the Practice of Travel Medicine (2012)*.

- Complete the CDC's *Yellow Fever Vaccine Course*.

- Have current <u>basic life support certification</u>.

- Complete <u>two hours of CE</u> focused on travel medicine (separate from CE on immunizations and vaccines) <u>every two years</u>.

Furnishing travel medications requires that the pharmacist follow these steps:

- Provide a "<u>good faith evaluation</u>" and assess the travel needs according to the patient's health status and the destinations they will visit. The travel history must include all the information necessary for a risk assessment during a pre-travel consultation; this is outlined in the CDC's *Yellow Book*.[154]

- Notify the patient's PCP of the drugs dispensed within <u>14 days</u> of furnishing, or enter the information in a shared record system, or provide the patient with a written record of the drugs received to provide to a PCP of their choice.

- Provide the patient with a <u>written record</u> of the drugs provided.

152   Self-treatable travel-related conditions are described in the CDC's Health Information for International Travel (commonly called the Yellow Book).
153   B&PC 4052(a)(10)(A)(3)
154   http://www.pharmacy.ca.gov/publications/travel_health_history_form.pdf (accessed 2018 Feb 16).

## PROVIDING CLINICAL SERVICES

### CLIA-Waived Tests

A pharmacist can perform <u>blood glucose</u>, hemoglobin <u>A1C</u> (referred to as A1C) and <u>cholesterol</u> tests that are waived under the <u>Clinical Laboratory Improvement Amendments</u> (CLIA); no California Department of Public Health (CDPH) registration is required. All other CLIA waived clinical laboratory tests require CDPH registration.

### Physical Assessments

Healthcare provider status broadens the pharmacists' scope of practice as members of the interdisciplinary healthcare team in all settings. This enables pharmacists to perform physical assessments as part of an initial patient assessment interview, or to monitor drug treatment. See the RxPrep Course Book chapter on Patient Charts, Assessment & Healthcare Provider Communication for further discussion.

Documentation is <u>required</u> for patient assessment, including results from the initial interview, monitoring appointments, referrals—for every step of the process. Adequate documentation improves the quality of care and permits appropriate continuation of care, such as required follow-ups and referrals.

---

**PHYSICAL ASSESSMENT**

**Conduct Patient Interview**
The physical assessment begins with an interview in a space that protects <u>patient privacy</u> and makes the patient feel comfortable. To establish rapport, the pharmacist should greet the patient by name, properly introduce themselves and explain their role and the purpose of the visit.

Questions should be <u>open-ended</u> unless a simple factual response is needed. Open-ended-questions require the patient to actually describe their complaints, giving much more accurate, patient-specific information than closed-ended questions. An open-ended question can begin with *"Tell me about…,"* *"Describe for me…,"* or *"Explain to me…"* An example of an open-ended question for a patient complaining of dizziness is *"Can you describe what you were doing before you became dizzy?"*

<u>Closed-ended</u> questions are answered with a <u>simple, one-word response</u>. An example of a closed-ended question would be *"Do you feel dizzy when you first get out of bed in the morning or if you stand up suddenly?"* The patient would answer with a "yes" or "no." Closed-ended questions can be appropriate when confirming information.

Active listening is required for a successful interview. Listening carefully to the patient conveys compassion and provides more insightful responses. Simple acknowledgements to demonstrate listening or understanding can be useful, such as *"I can see that"* or *"Anyone would feel anxious about that."* Avoid writing down notes or typing while the patient is speaking since this can be interpreted as a lack of complete attention. Observe the patient's body language and physical appearance to assess if the patient seems well, or appears energetic, tired or anxious.

**Obtain Health History, with Medication Use**
The health history includes the chief complaint (CC), the history of the present illness (HPI), the past medical history (PMH), the social history, the family history (first-degree relatives), allergies, intolerances and reactions, and medication use. The social history should include alcohol, tobacco and illicit (recreational) drug use. The medication use should include OTC medications and dietary or other supplements.

If the patient is a current tobacco user and is willing to try tobacco cessation, the pharmacist should counsel using the 5 A's Model. Counseling and medication use should be recommended in combination. Both approaches, when used together, achieve higher quit rates.

---

## PHYSICAL ASSESSMENT

**Vital Sign Measurement: Blood Pressure, Heart Rate, Respiratory Rate, Temperature (and Pain)**
Vital signs (blood pressure, heart rate, respiratory rate, and temperature) are measurements of the human body's most basic functions and are useful in detecting and monitoring medical problems. The Joint Commission requires pain to be assessed as the 5th vital sign in all Joint Commission-accredited facilities, which includes hospitals.[120] Pain is not a "vital" sign, but the designation is meant to increase awareness of the necessity for routine assessment. Pain assessment is described further.

### Blood Pressure
Blood pressure (BP) that remains high for an extended period of time (hypertension) can lead to severe consequences, including heart failure, stroke and kidney failure. Low BP (hypotension) may not be a serious issue as long as the patient feels fine. However, orthostatic hypotension (e.g., a sudden drop in BP when standing up from sitting or lying down) is dangerous because of the subsequent dizziness and risk of falls. Sudden drops in BP due to low or high body temperature, infection, dehydration, bleeding or an allergic reaction are serious. See the Hypertension chapter in the RxPrep Course Book for a further discussion. Patients who are found to have BP outside of the normal range at a healthcare screening should be referred for medical care.

To measure BP accurately:

- Ask about recent <u>tobacco, alcohol, and caffeine</u>, which can increase BP. Advise patients not to smoke tobacco or drink alcohol/caffeine at least 30 minutes before having BP taken.

- BP should be measured after the patient has used the restroom to empty their bladder, and has <u>rested comfortably</u> for 5 minutes in a <u>chair that supports the back</u>, with the <u>feet resting on the floor</u>.

- Instruct the patient to sit and <u>refrain from talking</u> during the measurement. Do not measure over clothing that constricts the arm.

- The arm being measured should be resting on a table or armchair at the <u>same level as the heart</u>.

- Use a sphygmomanometer with a stethoscope, or an electronic BP machine with an appropriate size cuff.

- At the initial visit, take two readings (one in each arm), 1 – 2 minutes apart and record the average. At subsequent visits measure the arm with the higher pressure.

- In elderly patients, or if dizziness or lightheadedness is present, measure for orthostatic hypotension while the patient is standing. Take the standing measurement 1 – 2 minutes after the sitting measurement. Orthostatic hypotension is present if the SBP decreases at least 20 mmHg or if the DBP decreases at least 10 mmHg.

Sphygmomanometer technique:

- Select the proper size cuff.

- Wrap the cuff snugly around the arm with the marker on the cuff placed over the brachial artery. The lower part of the cuff should be above the elbow. Two fingers should fit snugly under the cuff.

- Place diaphragm or bell of stethoscope over the brachial artery and under the cuff.

- Pump the bulb until pressure is 30 mmHg above the estimated SBP.

- Slowly open the valve to allow the pressure to fall, while listening for the <u>Korotkoff sounds</u> (sound of blood flowing).

- The SBP is when the Korotkoff sounds first appear. If this is missed, begin again with a higher initial pressure.

- The DBP is when the Korotkoff sounds disappear.

- When finished, rapidly release the remaining pressure and remove the cuff.

### Heart Rate
A normal resting heart rate (HR) for adults is between <u>60 – 100 beats per minute</u> (BPM). A fast HR (tachycardia) can be due to hypoglycemia, infection, dehydration, anxiety, pain, hyperthyroidism, anemia, arrhythmia, shock, excessive caffeine intake or drug use.

Drugs that commonly cause tachycardia include stimulants (of all types, including weight loss and ADHD drugs), decongestants (oral, and nasal with > 3 days use), beta-agonist over-use (such as albuterol), bupropion, antipsychotics and theophylline, especially with toxicity. Any type of extreme emotional or physical stress, including benzodiazepine and opioid withdrawal, will cause tachycardia. Reflex tachycardia can be due to a decrease (or

## PHYSICAL ASSESSMENT

displacement) in blood volume, which causes the heart to compensate by increasing HR to replace the blood volume. This can occur with the use of hydralazine, nitrates and the dihydropyridine (DHP) calcium channel blockers that have a strong vasodilation effect, such as nifedipine IR.

A low HR (bradycardia) may be normal for people who are athletes or those who exercise frequently, or can be due to an arrhythmia, organophosphate poisoning (such as from pesticides), hyperkalemia, hypothyroidism or may be drug-induced. A higher drug level will correlate with a higher degree of bradycardia, which could be a sign of overdose.

Drugs that can cause a low HR include beta blockers, non-DHP calcium channel blockers, clonidine, digoxin, antiarrhythmics, including sotalol, amiodarone and dronedarone, the acetylcholinesterase inhibitors used for dementia such as donepezil, and guanfacine, including the newer ADHD formulation *Intuniv*.[155] The initiation of fingolimod (*Gilenya*) for multiple sclerosis requires first-dose monitoring for bradycardia. The bradycardia from fingolimod is transient and only occurs only when the drug is started or restarted.

To measure HR, place your index and middle fingers on the patient's radial artery (found on the wrist) to feel the radial pulse. Count the pulse for 30 seconds and double the number to determine the beats per minute.

### Respiratory Rate
A normal respiratory rate (RR) for adults is 12 – 20 breaths per minute. Respiration rates can increase with asthma, COPD, anxiety, stress, heart failure, pneumonia, sepsis, ketoacidosis or stimulant drug use. A low respiratory rate can be due to opioids or hypothyroidism.

Respiratory rate can be measured by watching and counting the number of times the patient's chest rises and falls for 30 seconds, and doubling the result to determine the breaths per minute.

### Temperature
Normal body temperature in a healthy adult can range from 97.8° F (36.5°C) to 99° F (37.2°C). High temperature (hyperthermia) can be caused by fever, trauma, cancer, blood disorders, immune disorders or drugs. Low temperature (hypothermia) can be caused by exposure to cold, excessive alcohol intake, hypothyroidism or hypoglycemia.

Temperature is usually determined by ear (tympanic) or mouth (oral) measurements. Rectal measurement is an alternative, but uncomfortable in most cases, and impractical in the pharmacy setting.

- Tympanic membrane temperatures are quick, safe, and reliable. Make sure the ear canal is clear of earwax before aiming the beam of the thermometer at the tympanic membrane. Wait 2 - 3 seconds until the temperature reading appears.

- Oral temperatures are preferred over rectal but are not recommended when patients are restless or unable to close their mouths. If using an electronic thermometer, place the disposable cover over the probe and insert the thermometer under the patient's tongue. Ask the patient to close both lips. A temperature reading usually takes about 10 seconds.

### Pain
Pain is subjective, and thus, the primary measurement for assessing pain is the patient's own report, along with behavioral observations. The patient should be asked to identify the onset and temporal pattern, the location, the description (using the patient's own words), the intensity (using a pain scale), and any aggravating or relieving factors. The pharmacist should record previous treatments and their effectiveness.

Pain assessment requires an adequate "psycho-social" evaluation, which includes an interview and assessment of the factors which could be contributing to the pain response. It is common for patients with chronic pain to have concurrent psychological and social concerns.

Findings from the physical assessment, and any neurological and diagnostic procedure results should be included.

The Wong-Baker FACES Pain Rating Scale (shown) is a common tool for patients to communicate pain level, or a temperature scale (from green for no pain to red for the worst pain) or a simple numeric scale can be used. See the Pain chapter of the RxPrep Course Book.

155  The newer hepatitis C drugs containing sofosbuvir (Solvadi, Harvoni) and daclatasvir (Daklinza) cause significant bradycardia when two are used together with amiodarone, with more severe symptoms in patients who are also on beta blockers.

**PHYSICAL ASSESSMENT**

**The Physical Exam**

When hand-washing is required, such as prior to the physical exam, wash hands in front of the patient and don gloves.[156]

Physical examinations involve inspection, palpation, percussion, and auscultation:

- Inspection is using visual observation to note any deformities or abnormalities in the patient's physical appearance.

- Palpation is using hands to examine the patient's body, such as palpating the upper right quadrant of the abdomen to assess the liver for size, tenderness and masses.

- Percussion is tapping fingers on the patient's body, listening to the sound produced to determine if the tissue is air-filled (tympanic, drum-like sound), fluid-filled (dull sound), or solid (dull sound). For example, dull sounds can indicate a solid mass such as a healthy liver, or the presence of ascites.

- Auscultation is listening to the internal sounds of the patient's body (commonly the heart, lung or bowel sounds), usually with a stethoscope.

## Health Screenings

The community pharmacy setting reaches more people than can be seen in medical offices and comes complete with trained healthcare professionals—the pharmacists. The pharmacy setting provides an opportunity to screen patients for health conditions. In addition to the community setting, some institutional pharmacies provide health screenings and other clinical services. Assessing body fat, blood pressure, cholesterol, blood glucose, tobacco use, bone density, and depression are performed through health screenings at California pharmacies. If the values from the health screenings are abnormal, the patient can be offered services or, if needed, referred for further medical evaluation.

**HEALTH SCREENINGS**

**Body Fat Analysis (BMI and Waist Circumference)**

Overweight and obesity is a health problem associated with increased morbidity and mortality. Body mass index (BMI) is based on height and weight; review the BMI calculations and classifications in the Calculations chapter. A normal BMI is 18.5 – 24.9 kg/m². Waist circumference is used with BMI. If most of the fat is around the waist, there is high risk, which is defined for adults as a waist size > 40 inches for males or > 35 inches for females.

**Blood Pressure Screening**

Measurement and assessment of blood pressure is described the Physical Assessments section.

---

156   http://www.cdc.gov/handhygiene/ (accessed 2018 Feb 16).

## HEALTH SCREENINGS

### Glucose Screening

The ADA guidelines recommend testing for diabetes and prediabetes using A1C, FPG, or 2-hr plasma glucose after a 75-g OGTT. Using an OGTT is not practical in a community pharmacy setting. FPG testing is less expensive and can be used, but it requires the patient to fast for 8+ hours for accurate results. Patients at health screenings are generally not fasting. A1C testing does not require fasting and provides an accurate long-term blood glucose reading, but is more expensive.

Screening can be offered to all adults ages 45 years and older, and in adults of any age who are overweight or obese (BMI ≥ 25 for the general population or ≥ 23 in Asian Americans) with ≥ 1 risk factor. The pharmacist should review the medications for any that can contribute to hyperglycemia. Additional risk factors for cardiovascular disease (CVD) should be identified for treatment.

Glucose screening technique:

- Always wear gloves when working with blood or body fluid samples; change gloves between each patient
- Insert a test strip into glucose meter
- Calibrate the glucose meter with control solution if necessary
- Have patient warm up their hands; let the arm hang down at the person's side briefly to allow blood flow to the finger tips, either have the patient wash hands with warm soapy water or wipe fingertip with an alcohol swab and let dry
- Prick the side of the fingertip (or alternate testing site, depending on the meter used) with a lancet
- Squeeze the fingertip to aid blood flow, if needed
- Touch one edge of the test strip to the drop of blood which gets drawn up into the test strip
- Have the patient apply pressure to the puncture site until bleeding stops
- Apply a bandage to the puncture site
- Record glucose reading
- Dispose of properly; lancets should be placed into a sharps container

### Cholesterol Screening

Cholesterol screenings are available at most community pharmacies. *CardioChek* is a cholesterol measuring device that meets the National Cholesterol Education Program (NCEP) standards for accuracy, and is a small, hand-held device. See the Dyslipidemia chapter for cholesterol value interpretation.

Cholesterol screening technique using *CardioChek*:

- Always wear gloves when working with blood or body fluid samples; change gloves between each patient
- Insert the code chip that matches the lot of the test strips
- Insert test strip (avoid touching sample site)
- Have the patient warm up their hands; let the arm hang down at the person's side briefly to allow blood flow to the finger tips, either have the patient wash hands with warm soapy water or wipe fingertip with an alcohol swab and let dry
- Prick the side of the fingertip with a lancet
- Squeeze the fingertip to aid blood flow, if needed
- Wipe away the first drop of blood with gauze and use the second blood drop for testing
- Touch end of capillary tube/pipette to the second drop of blood
- To avoid gaps and air bubbles in the capillary tube/pipette, position the capillary tube/pipette so it is slightly tilted upward
- Repeat as needed to fill the capillary tube/pipette with blood (cholesterol screening requires a larger blood sample volume compared to glucose screening)
- Insert plunger into capillary tube (no assembly needed for a capillary pipette)
- Place capillary tube with the inserted plunger (or capillary pipette) over test strip blood application window
- Hold the capillary tube/pipette slightly above the blood application window, making sure to avoid touching the surface of the strip.
- Gently press the plunger down (or gently squeeze the bulb of the capillary pipette) to move the blood onto the test strip
- Have the patient apply pressure to the puncture site until bleeding stops, apply a bandage to the puncture site
- Results appear in ~2 minutes, record cholesterol reading
- Dispose of properly; lancets should be placed into a sharps container

## HEALTH SCREENINGS

**Bone Density Screening**
Pharmacies can offer bone density screenings with an ultrasound densitometer that measures the bone density in the heel. The densitometer is portable, quick, lacks x-ray emission, and provides the T-score. The gold standard for measuring bone density is the dual-energy X-ray absorptiometry (DXA) scan. Since the DXA scan emits radiation and is large, it is not practical to use a DXA scan in the pharmacy setting. If it is determined that the patient has low bone density using an ultrasound densitometer, the patient should be referred for a physician consult and a DXA scan. Diagnostic criteria are discussed in the Osteoporosis chapter of the RxPrep Course Book.

Screening for osteoporosis can be performed with an ultrasound densitometer following these steps:

- Have patient sit down and remove shoe and sock from the foot that will be tested
- Apply gel to machine and bare heel, if necessary
- Place patient's heel in machine
- Membranes will fill with warm water and surround heel and ankle
- Results appear in ~1 minute, record reading
- Wipe off excess gel and clean membranes

**Depression Screening**
The incidence of adult depression is between 3 – 5%. Increasingly, pharmacists are adding depression screening to MTM reviews. Screening for depression consists of asking the patient a series of questions, which is then scored.

Patients at risk for depression include those with substance abuse, other mental health conditions, pain, cancer or heart disease. In the elderly, long-term health changes that impair functional level increases risk for depression, as does loneliness, grief, and insomnia. Women who are pregnant or postpartum are at risk for depression and should be screened. Women and younger adults have higher risk.

There are several recommended screening forms that have been well-validated and which vary based on patient group.[157] The one used commonly for adults, the Patient Health Questionnaire (PHQ-9) is a simple check-off form that correlates to a score that indicates depression risk. [158]

**Tobacco Screening**
Screening for tobacco use should be done routinely, and should be part of a more comprehensive MTM review. This practice will identify many smokers; 16.8% of the adult population in the U.S. smoke cigarettes. Tobacco cessation is discussed previously. SB 493 authorizes pharmacists to furnish prescription NRT to patients.

## QUALITY ASSURANCE PROGRAMS

### National Patient Safety Goals

The purpose of The Joint Commission's National Patient Safety Goals (NPSGs) is to foster improvements in patient safety in Joint Commission-accredited facilities. The NPSGs highlight problematic areas in healthcare (such as the lack of consistently following CDC hand hygiene recommendations, or harm from the improper use of anticoagulants). Each NPSG targets one area and recommends steps to improve safety and reduce risk. Refer to the Medication Safety & Quality Improvement chapter for further discussion.

---

157  Effective depression screening tests in addition to PHQ-9 include the Hospital Anxiety and Depression Scales (for adults, inpatient), the Geriatric Depression Scale (for older adults), and the Edinburgh Postnatal Depression Scale (for postpartum and pregnant women).
158  http://www.cqaimh.org/pdf/tool_phq9.pdf (accessed 2018 Feb 21).

## Standard Order Sets

The use of standard order sets can promote best practice, decrease medication errors, improve workflow, improve patient outcomes, and standardize patient care.[159] Standard order sets reduce the need to call prescribers for clarification about an order.

Standard order sets have benefit only when they are developed carefully and are implemented at the facility. They should be evidence-based. Standard order sets should not include non-formulary medications, drugs withdrawn from the market, or equipment no longer available at the facility. Baseline tests and the frequency of monitoring must be defined, and when emergency treatment (such as the use of reversal agents with anticoagulants) is required. The figure shows part of a standard order set for administering potassium to treat hypokalemia.

| Current Serum Potassium Level | Central IV Administration | Peripheral IV Administration | Monitoring |
|---|---|---|---|
| 3.6 – 3.9 mEq/L | 20 mEq IV over 2 HR x 1 | 10 mEq IV over 1 HR x 2 | No additional action |
| 3.4 – 3.5 mEq/L | 20 mEq IV over 2 HR x 1 **AND** 10 mEq IV over 1 HR x 1 | 10 mEq IV over 1 HR x 3 | No additional action |
| 3.1 – 3.3 mEq/L | 20 mEq IV over 2 HR x 2 | 10 mEq IV over 1 HR x 4 | Recheck serum potassium level 2 hours after infusion complete |
| 2.6 – 3 mEq/L | 20 mEq IV over 2 HR x 2 **AND** 10 mEq IV over 1 HR x 1 | 10 mEq IV over 1 HR x 5 | Recheck serum potassium level 2 hours after infusion complete |
| 2.3 – 2.5 mEq/L | 20 mEq IV over 2 HR x 3 | 10 mEq IV over 1 HR x 6 | Recheck serum potassium level 2 hours after infusion complete |
| < 2.3 mEq/L | **Call Physician AND** 20 mEq IV over 2 HR x 3 | **Call Physician AND** 10 mEq IV over 1 HR x 6 | Recheck serum potassium level 2 hours after infusion complete |

- If both potassium and phosphorus replacement required, subtract the mEq of potassium given as potassium phosphate from total amount of potassium required. (Conversion: 3 mmols $KPO_4$ = 4.4 mEq $K^+$)
- Call pharmacy for assistance if needed.

## Antimicrobial Stewardship Programs

Antibiotics (antimicrobials) have transformed the practice of medicine by turning once lethal infections into manageable conditions. Like all medications, antibiotics have potentially serious adverse events, and are often overused/misused. The misuse of antibiotics contributes to the spread of antibiotic resistance and the creation of "superbugs". Superbugs are strains of bacteria that are resistant to several types of antibiotics. Some fatal superbugs are untreatable with the antibiotics available today.

Antibiotic stewardship programs (ASPs) ensure that hospitalized patients receive the right antibiotic, at the right dose, at the right time, and for the right duration.[160] Culture and susceptibility data can be used to determine the antibiotic with the narrowest possible spectrum for continuation of therapy. Using antibiotics appropriately will reduce antibiotic resistance and the evolution of superbugs. Please review the RxPrep Infectious Disease chapters for the appropriate use of antibiotics.

159  http://www.ismp.org/tools/guidelines/standardordersets.pdf (accessed 2018 Feb 16).
160  http://www.cdc.gov/getsmart/healthcare/evidence.html (accessed 2018 Feb 16).

## Medication Utilization Evaluation

The American Society of Health System Pharmacy (ASHP) defines medication-use evaluation (MUE) as a "performance improvement method that focuses on evaluating and improving medication-use processes with the goal of optimal patient outcomes".[161] In other words, it is a process to improve the use of drugs to increase the health benefit for patients. MUEs are often conducted in individual institutions, and sometimes as part of a larger effort to improve care across healthcare systems. MUE can be conducted for a specific drug (e.g., morphine), or for a drug class (e.g., opioids), a disease state (e.g., pain) or a process (such as prescribing, dispensing, or administration).

It can be interdisciplinary (involve the nurses, physicians, pharmacists, others) in order to achieve the best results, and have the recommendations implemented. It is important to identify ways to use the drugs safely and ensure that the facility follows the recommendations. The MUE process involves collecting and analyzing the events, improving software to avoid future events, and developing the action plan, which can include a standard order sets and treatment pathway.

An MUE can be used when a drug is especially toxic, when it is used in a group at high risk of ADRs (such as pediatrics), if the medication is being considered for addition to or removal from the formulary, or to identify poor and/or costly prescribing habits. The purposes for a MUE include: determining optimal medication therapy, preventing medication-related problems, evaluating the efficacy of a medication, and improving patient safety.

## Peer Review and Self Evaluation

A performance evaluation process conducted by peers and/or self is part of the quality assurance process. Evaluation can include standard objective criteria, and position-specific criteria. Peer experts are commonly involved in establishing competencies required for granting privileges, such as granting some type of practice designation, or the use of a high-risk agent. The standards involved with any type of privilege is continually updated, as needed.

---

161   https://www.ashp.org/-/media/assets/policy-guidelines/docs/guidelines/medication-use-evaluation.ashx (accessed 2018 Feb 16).

## Medication Error Reporting

Although pharmacists practice with the best intentions, medication errors occur, with the most common in the community pharmacy occurring when the wrong medication is dispensed to a patient. It is estimated that the overall dispensing accuracy rate in community pharmacy is 98.3%, which is ~4 errors per 250 prescriptions, according to the Institute for Safe Medication Practices (ISMP). California requires all pharmacies to have a quality assurance (QA) program to document, assess, and prevent medication errors. There must be a readily-retrievable P&P for the QA program so the pharmacy staff knows what to do when a medication error happens.

Investigation of pharmacy medication errors must begin within 2 business days from the date the medication error was discovered; otherwise, the sequence of events leading up to the event will be forgotten. The sooner the incident is documented, the better. Preferably, and especially if the consequences of the error are severe, the assessment should be conducted using a root cause analysis (RCA) to discover the causes in the system (i.e., the dispensing process) that led to the error, with the goal of designing changes to the system in order to avoid future repeats. RCA is discussed in more detail in the Medication Safety & Quality Improvement chapter of the RxPrep Course Book. The record of the QA review should be immediately retrievable in the pharmacy (i.e., it cannot be stored off-site) and must be kept in the pharmacy for at least 1 year from the date it was created. The record must contain the following information:

- Date, location, and participants in the QA review

- Pertinent data and other information related to the medication error

- Findings and determinations

- Recommended changes to pharmacy policy, procedure, systems or processes to avoid a repeat of the medication error

The pharmacist must inform the patient that a medication error has occurred and should inform the patient of any steps that can be taken to avoid further injury (such as the use of another agent to lessen the effects of a drug taken in error). The pharmacist must inform the prescriber that a medication error has occurred. The pharmacist should never attempt to cover up errors; it is accepted that pharmacists are human, and humans are fallible. The goal is to take care of the patient, and improve the workplace to limit future occurrences.

## PROMOTING PUBLIC HEALTH

### Medicare Part D

Medicare is federal health insurance for people ages ≥ 65 or < 65 with disability, and patients with end stage renal disease (ESRD). Medicare Part D is the drug benefit for Medicare enrollees. Medicare enrollees can apply for a low income subsidy (LIS), which pays for the Part D monthly premium, the annual deductible, and medication copays.

In addition to federal Medicare, lower income children, pregnant women, families and low income adults may be able to qualify for state Medicaid. Enrollees in Medicaid do not have copays. In California, the state Medicaid is called Medi-Cal.

All Medicare recipients in California are able to obtain drugs at the Medi-Cal reimbursement rate. There are Medicare plans with prescription drug coverage, including many of the Medicare Advantage plans, which are offered by private companies as alternatives to traditional Medicare.

Medicare uses a Star Rating System (on a scale of 1 to 5 stars) to determine how well Medicare Advantage and Medicare Part D prescription drug plans perform. Plans with higher ratings get perks, such as year-round open enrollment (versus once yearly enrollment), and financial bonuses.[162] Medicare Part D ratings are based on several quality measures, and can change from year to year.[163, 164] Quality measures related to drug therapy include:[165]

1. Annual comprehensive medication review (CMR) for patients enrolled in a medication therapy management (MTM) program. Pharmacists providing CMRs can use three CPT for billing when there is face-to-face MTM. The codes document the service, and can be used to bill any health plan that includes Medicare Part D.

2. Adherence to non-insulin diabetes medications, statins, and renin angiotensin system antagonists (including ACE inhibitors, ARBs and aliskiren).

3. Appropriate use or avoidance of high-risk medications in patients 65 years and older.

4. Ensuring statin use in patients with diabetes age 40 to 75 years old.

162   https://www.gao.gov/modules/ereport/handler.php?1=1&path=/ereport/GAO-13-279SP/data_center_savings/
      Health/27._Medicare_Advantage_Quality_Bonus_Payment_Demonstration (accessed 2018 Feb 16).
163   https://www.cms.gov/Medicare/Prescription-Drug-Coverage/PrescriptionDrugCovGenIn/Downloads/2017-Measure-
      List.pdf (accessed 2018 Feb 16).
164   https://www.cms.gov/Medicare/Prescription-Drug-Coverage/PrescriptionDrugCovGenIn/Downloads/2017_Techni-
      cal_Notes_preview_1_2016_08_03.pdf (accessed 2018 Feb 16).
165   https://pqaalliance.org/measures/cms.asp (accessed 2018 Feb 16).

## Covered California

Covered California is the name of the health insurance "marketplace" in California. This includes a website where patients can compare the different Affordable Care Act (ACA) plans and enroll for coverage. All of the plans offered through Covered California provide prescription drugs, which are included as one of the "essential health benefits" that the ACA plans must include, in addition to contraception, described previously, and other services.[166]

Covered California was launched in 2014. Covered California plans are sold in four levels of coverage: Bronze, Silver, Gold and Platinum. For patients under 30 years of age, another option, called the minimum coverage plan, is also available. The higher-cost plans pay a higher percentage of covered medical expenses, compared with what a patient would be expected to pay in copays and annual deductibles.

Patients should enroll in plans based on their individual health needs. A young, healthy person may choose to enroll in the minimum coverage plan or bronze plan since this person only anticipates going to the doctor once a year for an annual check-up. A patient with several comorbidities, requires expensive speciality drugs, and regular follow-up visits with a specialist may find it more cost-effective to enroll in a platinum plan. Even though the platinum plan has a relatively higher monthly premium, the co-pay for doctor visits and prescription drugs are lower than the bronze plan.

## Patient Assistance Programs

Patient assistance programs (PAPs) help low-income, uninsured patients get free or low-cost, brand-name medications. These programs are typically provided by the pharmaceutical manufacturer that makes the drug. There are several online directories that help patients find a specific patient assistance program, including the popular RxAssist site at www.rxassist.org.

This is the page from the RxAssist website for the company *Sanofi*. If the requirements are met, the patient can qualify for *Sanofi* drugs at no cost.

**Eligibility Info:**
- This program offers Reimbursement, Resource and Patient Assistance information.
- Must not have prescription coverage and must not be eligible for state or federal programs such as Medicare and Medicaid.
- For most medications (excluding Lovenox) patients with Medicare Part D might be considered if they are ineligible for Low Income Subsidy and have spent at least 5% of their annual household income (out of pocket) on medications.
- Patient must be under the care of a licensed healthcare provider who is authorized to prescribe, dispense, and administer medicine in the US.
- For Vaccines, patient must be at least 19 years of age.

166  https://www.coveredca.com/individuals-and-families/getting-covered/coverage-basics/essential-health-benefits/ (accessed 2018 Feb 16).

### Tablet Splitting

Splitting tablets can <u>save patients money</u>. Health plans can also save money because manufacturers sometimes charge the same price for higher and lower doses of the same drug.

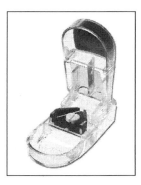

The easiest tablets to split are the ones that are <u>scored</u>. Patients should use commercially available devices ("pill cutters" or "pill splitters") specifically designed to split tablets. Patients should not use a kitchen knife or other tools that can result in an uneven split or accidently hurt the patient. Split tablets can deteriorate and lose their effectiveness when exposed to air and moisture for too long; so splitting should occur close to the time the split dose is needed.[167]

Not all drugs can be safely or practically split. There are some tablets that <u>crumble easily</u> and others that are <u>coated</u> to protect the GI lining or to prevent the drug from degrading in the stomach. Patients with <u>manual dexterity problems</u> (e.g., arthritis, Parkinson's disease), <u>visual impairment</u>, or <u>cognitive impairment</u> are not good candidates for tablet splitting. Do not advise patients to split very small tablets, asymmetrical tablets, narrow therapeutic index drugs, capsules, enteric-coated tablets, film-coated tablets, or extended-release tablets.[168] There are no California laws or pharmacy regulations specifically forbidding tablet splitting. The pharmacist and patient should decide whether splitting tablets is appropriate.

### Other Drug Cost-Saving Strategies

There are other ways a pharmacist can advise a patient to save money on drugs:[169]

- The same drug can be less expensive at a different pharmacy; it may be useful to do a cost comparison.

- Consider using the <u>generic</u> equivalent of a brand name drug.

- Suggest to the prescriber a <u>therapeutically similar but less expensive drug</u>. Keep in mind that drugs in advertisements are new and generally more expensive than older alternatives.

- Consider purchasing a <u>greater day supply</u> (90-day instead of a 30-day) if the copay is the same.

167   http://www.pharmacy.ca.gov/publications/pill_splitting_brochure.pdf (accessed 2018 Feb 16).
168   http://www.pharmacy.ca.gov/publications/07_jul_script.pdf (accessed 2018 Feb 16).
169   http://www.pharmacy.ca.gov/publications/discount_rx_facts.pdf (accessed 2018 Feb 16).

# 3

# Regulation of Controlled Substances

The next section reviews the Controlled Substances Act. The regulations previously discussed for all drugs also apply to controlled substances, and there are additional regulations and requirements as well. The federal Drug Enforcement Administration (DEA) and the board collaborate to enforce the controlled substances laws. The following table contains important DEA forms which will be discussed throughout this section:

| DEA FORM # | PURPOSE |
|---|---|
| 224 | Registration Form for Retail Pharmacies, Hospitals/Clinics, Practitioners, Teaching Institutions, or Mid-Level Practitioners |
| 225 | Registration Form for Manufacturers, Distributors, Researchers, Analytical Laboratories, Importers, Exporters |
| 363 | Registration Form for Narcotic Treatment Programs |
| 222 | Ordering Schedule I and II Drugs |
| 106 | Reporting the Theft or Significant Loss of Controlled Substances |
| 41 | Record of Controlled Substances Destroyed |

## DRUG ENFORCEMENT AGENCY REGISTRANTS

DEA registration is required with every step in the closed system of controlled substance movement and ends when the drug is dispensed or administered to the patient. If an individual or business/facility wants to be involved with manufacturing, distributing, prescribing, dispensing, or disposal of controlled substances, the individual needs to register with the DEA.

Individual prescribers and institutions (including prescribers, hospitals and pharmacies) submit the DEA Form 224 to apply for a DEA number.[170] Manufacturers and distributors of drugs register with the DEA Form 225.

---

170   http://www.deadiversion.usdoj.gov/drugreg/reg_apps/224/224_instruct.htm (accessed 2018 Jan 25).

## CLASSIFICATION OF CONTROLLED SUBSTANCES

The DEA works with the Food and Drug Administration to place <u>controlled substances</u> into <u>five different schedules</u>, based on the <u>accepted medical use</u>, potential for <u>abuse</u>, and potential to create severe <u>psychological</u> and/or <u>physical dependence</u>. Sometimes, a drug is moved to a different schedule (such as the recent move of all hydrocodone-containing products into schedule II) if the perceived risks involving a drug has changed. States have their own authority under controlled substances regulations and may classify substances in stricter categories (e.g., paregoric is classified as schedule III at the federal level, but classified as schedule II at the state level). Whenever there is a discrepancy between federal and state law, the <u>stricter</u> law prevails.

The higher the potential for abuse, the lower the schedule number. <u>Schedule I</u> drugs have the <u>highest potential for abuse</u> and are considered to have <u>no accepted medical use</u>. Drugs in this category (such as heroin and LSD) may be used for research purposes, but are most commonly used illicitly (illegally/unlawfully). Marijuana is an exception; it is classified as schedule I according to the DEA, but is available for medicinal and adult recreational use in California.[171] Marijuana is not dispensed in pharmacies and remains illegal under federal law. The DEA has not strictly enforced this law.

Some drugs can be classified in <u>more than one schedule</u> depending on the <u>formulation</u>. Codeine is schedule II if it is a single agent, schedule III if formulated as part of a combination tablet/capsule, and schedule V if formulated as a combination cough syrup. Dronabinol is schedule II as a solution and schedule III as a capsule. In contrast, hydrocodone is schedule II in all single and combination products and tramadol is schedule IV in all single and combination products as well.

Generally, most controlled substances of the <u>same pharmacological class</u> will be in the <u>same schedule</u>. For example, benzodiazepines are generally schedule IV. However, barbiturates can be schedule II, III, or IV. Single agent formulations of amobarbital, pentobarbital, secobarbital are schedule II. If amobarbital, secobarbital, or pentobarbital is formulated as a suppository or as a combination product with a non-controlled substance, then it becomes schedule III. Butabarbital is schedule III. Butabarbital is not to be confused with butalbital. Butalbital is currently only available as a combination product with non-controlled substances and is schedule III. Phenobarbital is schedule IV. Phenobarbital is not to be confused with pentobarbital.

| SCHEDULE | EXAMPLES |
|---|---|
| C-I | 3,4-methylenedioxymethamphetamine or MDMA |
| | Gamma-hydroxybutyric acid or GHB (the sodium salt form, sodium oxybate, is C-III) |
| | Heroin |
| | Lysergic acid diethylamide or LSD |
| | Marijuana or *cannabis* (tetrahydrocannabinol, cannabidiol) |
| | Mescaline |
| | Peyote |

171   *The Adult Use of Marijuana Act*

| SCHEDULE | EXAMPLES |
|----------|----------|
| C-II | Alfentanyl (*Alfenta*) |
| | Amobarbital (*Amytal Sodium*) |
| | Amphetamine (*Dyanavel, Evekeo*) |
| | Amphetamine/Dextroamphetamine (*Adderall, Adderall XR*) |
| | Cocaine |
| | Codeine |
| | Dexmethylphenidate (*Focalin, Focalin XR*) |
| | Dextroamphetamine (*Dexedrine, ProCentra, Zenzedi*) |
| | Dronabinol solution (*Syndros*) |
| | Fentanyl (*Duragesic, Actiq, Fentora, Subsys, Lazanda, Abstral*) |
| | Hydrocodone containing products (*Zohydro ER, Hysingla ER, Norco, Vicodin, Hycet, Lortab, TussiCaps, Tussionex, Vicoprofen, Xodol*) |
| | Hydromorphone (*Dilaudid, Exalgo*) |
| | Levo-alpha acetyl methadol or LAAM |
| | Levorphanol |
| | Lisdexamfetamine (*Vyvanse*) |
| | Meperidine (*Demerol*) |
| | Methadone (*Dolophine, Methadose, Methadone HCl Intensol*) |
| | Methamphetamine (*Dexosyn*) |
| | Methylphenidate (*Ritalin, Ritalin LA, Concerta, Cotempla XR-ODT, Methylin, QuilliChew ER, Quillivant XR, Aptensio XR, Metadate ER, Daytrana*) |
| | Morphine (*MS Contin, Kadian, Duramorph, Arymo ER, MorphaBond ER, Infumorph*) |
| | Oxycodone containing products (*Percocet, Percodan, Endodan, Endocet, OxyCONTIN, Roxicodone, Oxaydo, Xartemis XR, Xtampza ER*) |
| | Oxymorphone (*Opana*) |
| | Paregoric |
| | Pentobarbital (*Nembutal*) |
| | Secobarbital (*Seconal*) |
| | Sufentanil |
| | Tapentadol (*Nucynta*) |
| C-III | Anabolic steroids such as testosterone (*AndroGel, Androderm, Testim, Fortesta, Depo-Testosterone*) |
| | Benzphetamine (*Regimex*) |
| | Buprenorphine containing products (*Belbuca, Buprenex, Butrans, Probuphine Implant Kit, Sublocade, Suboxone, Zubsolv, Bunavail*) |
| | Butabarbital (*Butisol*) |
| | Butalbital-containing products (*Allzital, Bupap, Marten-Tab, Fioricet, Fioricet with Codeine, Fiorinal, Fiorinal with Codeine*) |
| | Codeine/acetaminophen (*Tylenol with Codeine #3, Tylenol with Codeine #4*) |
| | Dronabinol capsules (*Marinol*) |
| | Ketamine (*Ketalar*) |
| | Phendimetrazine |
| | Sodium oxybate (*Xyrem*) |

| SCHEDULE | EXAMPLES |
|---|---|
| C-IV | Armodafinil (*Nuvigil*) |
| | Benzodiazepines such as lorazepam (*Ativan*), diazepam (*Valium*), alprazolam (*Xanax*) |
| | Butorphanol (*Stadol*) |
| | Carisoprodol (*Soma*) |
| | Diethylpropion |
| | Difenoxin/atropine (*Motofen*) |
| | Eluxadoline (*Viberzi*) |
| | Eszopiclone (*Lunesta*) |
| | Lorcaserin (*Belviq*) |
| | Modafinil (*Provigil*) |
| | Phenobarbital |
| | Phentermine (*Adipex-P, Lomaira*) |
| | Phentermine/topiramate (*Qsymia*) |
| | Suvorexant (*Belsomra*) |
| | Tramadol containing products (*Ultram, Ultracet, ConZip*) |
| | Zaleplon (*Sonata*) |
| | Zolpidem (*Ambien, Ambien CR, Edluar, Intermezzo, Zolpimist*) |
| C-V | Brivaracetam (*Briviact*) |
| | Codeine containing cough syrups (codeine/promethazine, codeine/promethazine/phenylephrine, codeine/guaifenisen, others) |
| | Difenoxin/atropine (*Motofen half strength*) – discontinued |
| | Diphenoxylate/atropine (*Lomotil*) |
| | Ezogabine |
| | Lacosamide (*Vimpat*) |
| | Pregabalin (*Lyrica*) |

## ORDERING CONTROLLED SUBSTANCES

Because schedule II drugs have the highest potential for abuse, there are stricter regulations on how to order them. Schedule II drugs can be ordered with a Form 222 or through the Controlled Substance Ordering System (CSOS).

To order schedule III – V drugs, the pharmacy must use a purchase order and keep a receipt (invoice or packing slip) on which it records the date the drugs were received and confirms that the order is accurate. These receipts must contain the name of each controlled substance, the finished form, the number of dosage units of finished form in each commercial container, and the number of commercial containers ordered and received. In addition, these receipts must be maintained in a readily retrievable manner for inspection by the DEA. Schedule III – V drugs can also be ordered through CSOS.

## Ordering Schedule II Drugs with the DEA Form 222

A Form 222 or CSOS, it's electronic equivalent, is used to trace the movement of schedule II drugs. The Form 222 goes with each distribution, purchase or transfer and is used when the schedule II drugs move from the wholesaler/supplier to a pharmacy, from a pharmacy to another pharmacy, from a pharmacy to a DEA-sanctioned disposal facility, and, in some cases, back to the wholesaler if the drug is being returned. Schedule I drugs may be used for research with permission from the DEA and FDA but are not ordered by pharmacies nor prescribed by healthcare providers.

The registrant requesting/receiving the controlled substances (such as a pharmacy) will keep Copy 3 and send Copies 1 & 2 to the supplier. Upon delivery of the controlled substances to the pharmacy, the registrant supplying the drugs (which is generally the drug wholesaler) will send Copy 2 to the DEA. Note that the pharmacy keeps Copy 3 when purchasing the controlled substances from the wholesaler — but will keep Copy 1 when returning drugs to a wholesaler or reverse distributor since now the pharmacy is "supplying" the drugs. In this case, the pharmacy is responsible for sending Copy 2 to the DEA.

| ACTION | COPY 1 (BROWN) | COPY 2 (GREEN) | COPY 3 (BLUE) |
|---|---|---|---|
| The pharmacy orders schedule II drugs from a wholesaler | Supplier | DEA | Pharmacy |
| The pharmacy returns unused schedule II drugs back to a supplier | Pharmacy | DEA | Supplier |
| The pharmacy sends unused schedule II drugs back to reverse distributor for disposal | Pharmacy | DEA | Reverse distributor |
| The pharmacy sells or lends schedule II drugs to another pharmacy that is out of stock and needs the drugs to dispense a prescription | Supplying pharmacy | DEA | Receiving pharmacy |
| The pharmacy sells or lends schedule II drugs to a physician for administration or dispensing to a patient | Pharmacy | DEA | Physician |

A Form 222 is not required if the drugs are transferred from a central fill pharmacy to its retail pharmacy. Schedule II prescriptions cannot be transferred from pharmacy to pharmacy for the purposes of dispensing to a patient. The purpose of the Form 222 is to document every distribution, purchase, or transfer of schedule II drugs, except for the last step to the patient.

The Form 222 is serially numbered (with a consecutive number series) and is pre-printed with the pharmacy's name, address, DEA number, and the schedules of controlled substances that can be ordered by the registrant. The colors of the triplicate forms are brown (1st), green (2nd), and blue (3rd). If a DEA registration terminates for any reason, or if the preprinted name and address needs to be revised, the unused DEA forms are returned to the DEA and new forms, if needed, must be issued.

Initial DEA Forms 222 can be requested on the DEA Form 224, *Application for New Registration*. Once a registrant has received a DEA registration number, additional DEA Forms 222 may be ordered on the DEA website or by calling DEA Headquarters Registration Unit or the nearest DEA Registration Field Office.

These are the steps on how to order schedule II drugs with the Form 222:

1. A Form 222 is filled out with a typewriter, ink pen, or indelible (non-erasable) pencil.

2. Each item must be written on a separate line with a maximum of 10 lines on each form; a maximum of 10 items can be ordered. Lines cannot be skipped.

3. The purchaser must fill out the name and address of the supplier. Only one supplier can be used on a form.

4. The purchaser can leave the NDC entry blank since the purchaser may not know which NDC the supplier has in stock.

5. The purchaser must enter the line number that contains the last drug ordered. This field must be completed and will be 10 or less. If this is left blank or does not match the number of lines used on the Form, it will be returned to the pharmacy.

6. The Form 222 must be signed and dated by the person authorized to sign the registration application or a person who has been granted power of attorney. If the form is not signed and dated, it will be returned to the pharmacy.

7. If a mistake is made, the purchaser must write "VOID" on the Form 222 and start over with a new Form 222.

8. The Form 222 must be filled out completely and must include the drug/s name, strength, size, quantity, and be signed with the date. If any of these items are missing, or if the form is sloppy and not legible, the Form 222 cannot be used by the supplier and will be returned to the purchaser. Minor errors could be reasonably corrected.

9. Once completed, the purchaser keeps Copy 3 (blue Copy), and sends Copies 1 and 2 (brown and green Copies) to the supplier. The first two Copies must remain together, with the carbon intact. If the top 2 Copies are not attached to each other, the supplier cannot accept the order and should return the Form 222 to the pharmacy.

10. On Copies 1 and 2 the supplier records the number of containers furnished for each item and the date of the shipment. If the supplier cannot provide the entire quantity, the supplier can provide a partial shipment and supply the balance within 60 days from the date on the Form. The supplier keeps Copy 1 for its files and sends Copy 2 to the DEA by the end of the month during which the order was fulfilled. If the supplier cannot fulfill the order within the specified time limit, the supplier may endorse the order over to another supplier to fill.

11. Shipments of controlled substances can only be delivered to the current DEA registered address.

12. The supplier delivers the scheduled drugs to the purchaser in its own containers, which must be in separate containers from the rest of the order. The supplier cannot pack the scheduled drugs with the non-controlled drugs or OTC products. When the order arrives at the pharmacy, it will be <u>checked in by a pharmacist</u>, who will record the <u>number of packages</u> and the <u>date received</u> on Copy 3 (the pharmacist checks the drugs received to their Copy from the original order.)

13. The purchaser must keep Copy 3 of the Form 222 (and all scheduled drug forms) for at least <u>3 years</u>. All records related to schedule II drugs (orders, invoices, prescriptions, inventory records) need to be kept separate from other forms.

### Cancelling or Voiding DEA Form 222

If the supplier cannot fulfill the order or if the order form is illegible, incomplete, or altered, then the supplier has to send back Copies 1 and 2 to the purchaser with a rationale for not filling the order. The purchaser must keep all three Copies.

A supplier can void part or all of an order by notifying the purchaser in writing. The supplier will draw a line through the cancelled items on Copies 1 and 2 and print "void" in the space where they would usually put the number of items shipped.

A purchaser can cancel all or part of an order on a Form 222 by notifying the supplier in writing. The supplier indicates the cancellation on Copies 1 and 2 by drawing a line through the cancelled item/s and writing "cancelled" in the space where they would usually put the number of items shipped.

### Lost or Stolen DEA Form 222

If a completed Form 222 is lost or stolen, the purchaser must re-order with a new Form 222. The serial number of the lost or stolen form, the date of loss, and a statement that the controlled substances were not received must be recorded on the new Form 222. A copy of this statement must be sent to the supplier, along with Copies 1 and 2 of the second order form. The purchaser files Copy 3 of the new and original lost or stolen Form 222 together. If the supplier subsequently receives the original order form, it is marked as "not accepted" and returned to the purchaser who files original Copies 1 and 2 with the original Copy 3.

## Ordering Schedule II – V Drugs with the Controlled Substance Order System

The Controlled Substance Order System (CSOS) is the electronic equivalent to Form 222 and is used to electronically order schedule II drugs — with a big difference: while Form 222 is only used to order schedule II drugs, CSOS can be used to order drugs from <u>all schedules</u> and can be used to order non-controlled drugs as well.[172]

---

172   www.deaecom.gov/overview.pdf (accessed 2018 Jan 26).

There are other benefits to CSOS. Each Form 222 can be used to order up to 10 items; CSOS has no quantity limits. Using CSOS reduces ordering errors, requires less paperwork, and cuts administrative costs. Drug delivery with CSOS is faster; a pharmacy can enter an order online, have the order reach the supplier the same day, and the order can get delivered the next business day. With CSOS, there is less consolidating of orders by pharmacists, and orders can be placed more often for fewer items.

| | PAPER DEA FORM 222 | ELECTRONIC CSOS |
|---|---|---|
| Maximum # of items per order | 10 items | No maximum |
| What drugs can be ordered | Schedule I, II | Schedule I, II, III, IV, V and non-scheduled drugs |
| Typical turnaround time | 1-7 business days | 1-2 business days |
| Type of signature used | Wet (handwritten) signature | Digital signature |
| Can the order be endorsed to another supplier? | Yes | No |
| When must supplier report transaction to DEA? | By the end of the month during which the order was filled | Within 2 business days of filling the order |

The registrant creates an electronic 222 order using DEA-approved software which is typically available through the wholesaler's online ordering website. When the order is complete, the purchaser signs it with the digital certificate and electronically transmits it to the supplier. The supplier receives the order, verifies the certificate, and fills the order. The supplier must report the order information to the DEA within 2 business days from the date the supplier filled it.

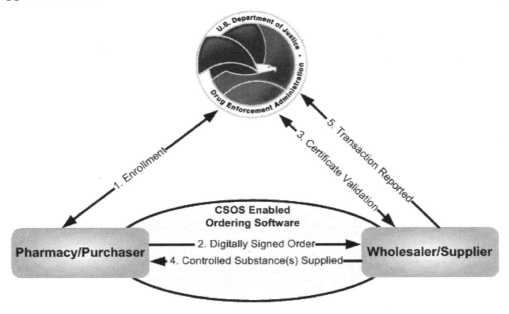

*Image courtesy of the Drug Enforcement Administration*

## Granting Power of Attorney for Form 222 and CSOS

The person who registered with the DEA to order controlled drugs using Form 222 or CSOS may not be present in the pharmacy at all times. Other staff members who are trustworthy and to whom the registrant has granted a power of attorney (POA) can order controlled substances. The POA is a written authorization permitting the other staff member/s, who can be licensed or unlicensed, to order controlled substances on behalf of the registrant. The registrant can issue multiple POA's if ordering will be done by multiple staff members. The registrant who issued the POAs can revoke them at any time. The POA is granted by the current DEA registrant; if another person at the pharmacy completes the DEA renewal application, new POA/s will need to be completed. The POA documents are not submitted to the DEA, but must be filed with the executed Form 222s and be readily retrievable in the event that the pharmacy needs to provide them to an inspector. The DEA does not provide an official POA form, but recommends the following wording:

---

**POWER OF ATTORNEY**

_____

(Name of registrant)

_____

(Address of registrant)

_____

(DEA registration number)

I, _____ (name of person granting power), the undersigned, who am authorized to sign the current application for registration of the above-named registrant under the Controlled Substances Act or Controlled Substances Import and Export Act, have made, constituted, and appointed, and by these presents, do make, constitute, and appoint _____ (name of attorney-in-fact), my true and lawful attorney for me in my name, place, and stead, to execute applications for Forms 222 and to sign orders for Schedule I and II controlled substances, whether these orders be on Form 222 or electronic, in accordance with 21 U.S.C. 828 and Part 1305 of Title 21 of the Code of Federal Regulations. I hereby ratify and confirm all that said attorney must lawfully do or cause to be done by virtue hereof.

_____

(Signature of person granting power)

I, _____ (name of attorney-in-fact), hereby affirm that I am the person named herein as attorney-in-fact and that the signature affixed hereto is my signature.

_____

(Signature of attorney-in-fact)

Witnesses:

1. _____    2. _____

Signed and dated on the _____ day of _____, (year), at _____.

NOTICE OF REVOCATION

The foregoing power of attorney is hereby revoked by the undersigned, who is authorized to sign the current application for registration of the above-named registrant under the Controlled Substances Act or the Controlled Substances Import and Export Act. Written notice of this revocation has been given to the attorney-in-fact _____ this same day.

_____

(Signature of person revoking power)

Witnesses:

1. _____    2. _____

Signed and dated on the _____ day of _____, (year), at _____.

---

## HEALTHCARE PROVIDERS AUTHORIZED TO PRESCRIBE CONTROLLED SUBSTANCES

A prescription for a controlled substance for a legitimate medical purpose may only be issued by a physician (MD/DO), dentist (DDS/DMD), podiatrist (DPM), veterinarian (DVM), mid-level practitioner (MLP), or other registered practitioner who is:

- Authorized to prescribe controlled substances by the jurisdiction or state in which the practitioner is licensed to practice

- Registered or exempt from DEA registration, which includes the U.S. Public Health Service, Federal Bureau of Prisons, Army, Navy, Marine Corps and Coast Guard

- An agent or employee of a hospital or institution acting in the normal course of business under the DEA registration of the hospital or institution

See table under "Healthcare Providers Authorized to Prescribe Medications" for details on the type of controlled substances various practitioners can prescribe.

### Checking the Validity of a DEA Number

After registering with the DEA, the registrant will be assigned a unique DEA number. Each DEA number begins with 2 letters, followed by 7 randomly-generated numbers. The last number is called a "check" digit since it is used to check that the DEA number may be legitimate.

The first letter identifies the type of registration:

| FIRST LETTER | TYPE OF DEA REGISTRATION |
|---|---|
| A, B, F, G | Hospital, clinic, practitioner, teaching institution, pharmacy |
| M | Mid-level practitioner (nurse practitioners, physician assistants, optometrists, etc.) |
| P, R | Manufacturer, distributor, researcher, analytical lab, importer, exporter, reverse distributor, narcotic treatment program |

The second letter of the DEA number is the first letter of the prescriber's last name. For example: Wendy Clark, MD has the DEA number AC2143799, where A is the initial letter (Dr. Clark is a physician), C is for her last name (Clark), followed by 7 numeric digits.

If a practitioner is authorized to prescribe narcotics (such as buprenorphine) for opioid addiction treatment, there will be a letter "X" that replaces the first letter. The provision that permits this prescribing is called "DATA 2000" and is described later in this manual. If Dr. Clark decided to take DATA 2000 training and could then prescribe for this purpose, her DATA 2000 waiver unique identification number (UIN) would be XC2143799. The UIN is in addition to a prescriber's DEA number and both numbers should be on the prescription.

Practitioners in a hospital or institution (such as medical interns, residents, or visiting physicians) who are acting in the normal course of business at the institution may prescribe medication under the DEA registration of that hospital or institution.

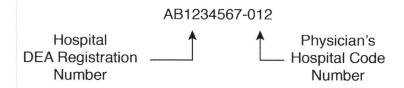

### Steps to Verify the Validity of a DEA Number

There are certain requirements the DEA number must meet in order to be valid. Pharmacists can use the following steps to verify the likely validity of a prescriber's DEA number.

---

Step one: Add the 1st, 3rd and 5th digits together.

Step two: Add the 2nd, 4th and 6th digits together.

Step three: Multiply the result of step two by 2.

Step four: Add the results of step one and three together, the last digit of this sum should match the last digit of the prescriber's DEA number. This is called the check digit.

Example: Dr. Thomas, DEA number BT6835752

Step one: 6 + 3 + 7 = 16

Step two: 8 + 5 + 5 = 18

Step three: 18 * 2 = 36

Step four: 16 + 36 = 52

The last digit of the sum of step four is 2, which is the same as the last digit of the DEA number. Therefore, this DEA number is valid.

Verify Dr. Mikacich's DEA number (B M 6 1 2 5 3 4 1) by completing the four steps after verifying that the first letter confers the ability to prescribe and the second letter matches the first letter of the last name.

Step one:

Step two:

Step three:

Step four:

The last digit of the sum of step four is _____.

Does Dr. Mikacich's DEA number appear to be valid? Yes/No

---

## REQUIREMENTS FOR VALID CONTROLLED SUBSTANCE PRESCRIPTIONS

All controlled substances prescriptions are valid for six months and must be <u>signed</u> and <u>dated</u> by the prescriber.[173] If the prescription is written for a <u>controlled</u> substance, the prescriber's <u>DEA number</u> must be included.

Any agent of the prescriber (e.g., nurse or office staff) can orally or electronically transmit a prescription for a controlled substance classified in Schedule III, IV, or V. The name of the agent transmitting the prescription is recorded.[174]

### Written Prescriptions (California Security Forms) for Controlled Substances

With the exception of prescriptions written for terminally ill patients[175] and for emergency use,[176] all written controlled substances prescriptions (Schedules II – V) must be written on <u>California security prescription forms</u>.[177]

A California security prescription form has the following features:

■ If a prescription is scanned or photocopied, the word "<u>void</u>" appears due to the heat exposure in a pattern across the entire front of the prescription.

■ A <u>chemical void protection</u> that prevents alteration via chemical washing.

■ A <u>watermark</u> is printed on the back of the prescription blank that reads "California Security Prescription." Watermarks are not duplicated by copy machines.

■ A feature printed in <u>thermochromic ink</u>. Thermochromic inks react to changes in temperature. Commonly, if a thermochromic image is touched or blowed on it will disappear, and will reappear after it cools. Thermochromic ink's effect is not duplicated by copy machines.

■ An area of <u>opaque writing</u> so that the writing disappears if the prescription is lightened.

■ A <u>description</u> of the security features included on each form.

■ Six <u>quantity check off boxes</u> printed on the form with the following quantities: 1-24, 25-49, 50-74, 75-100, 101-150, 151 and over. Along with the quantity boxes, a space must be provided to designate the <u>units</u> referenced in the quantity boxes when the drug is not in tablet or capsule form (e.g., mL).

■ Statement that the "Prescription is void if the number of drugs prescribed is not noted."

173   H&SC 11164(a)(1)
174   H&SC 11164(b)(3)
175   H&SC 11159.2
176   H&SC 11167
177   H&SC 11164(a)

- The <u>preprinted</u> name, category of licensure, license number, federal DEA registration number of the prescribing practitioner.

- <u>Check boxes</u> so that the prescriber can indicate the <u>number of refills</u> ordered.

- The date of issue.

- A <u>check box</u> indicating the prescriber's order <u>not to substitute</u>.

- An identifying number assigned to the approved security printer by the Department of Justice.

- A <u>check box</u> by the name of each prescriber when a prescription form lists <u>multiple prescribers</u>. A prescriber who signs a multiple prescriber form will need to check the box by his or her name.

Each batch of security prescription forms has a <u>lot number</u> printed on the form. The forms are printed sequentially, beginning with the number one.

Prescribers can write a prescription for both <u>controlled</u> and <u>non-controlled</u> drugs on the security forms, or they can choose to use separate forms for each type.

Security forms are also required for all <u>written Medi-Cal outpatient prescriptions</u> (including <u>over-the-counter</u> drugs, <u>non-controlled</u> drugs, and <u>controlled substances</u>). A prescriber can use a California security form for controlled substances to write prescriptions for Medi-Cal patients since it <u>exceeds</u> the Medi-Cal security requirements. See the Written Prescriptions for Medi-Cal Outpatient Drugs discussion in this manual.

There is an increasing number of inappropriate security forms being brought into pharmacies, and an increasing number of stolen security forms. The board posts on its website confirmed notices of stolen or compromised security prescription forms that have been reported by prescribers. A list of these can be viewed on the board's website.[178]

It is a pharmacist's responsibility to ensure that security forms are legitimate by confirming that the security features are present, and by confirming that the prescriber information is accurate. Pharmacists should be aware of red flags that signal a warning that abuse and diversion risk is present, which could include any missing security features or other red flags described later in this manual.

---

178   http://www.pharmacy.ca.gov/licensees/stolen_fraudulent_rx_forms.shtml (accessed 2018 Feb 16).

**Multiple Prescriber Forms for Hospitals and Other Institutions**

Hospitals often have physicians from the surrounding community who are granted privileges to see their patients at the hospital. Many hospitals have medical residents rotating through the facility for short periods of time. Both types of prescribers need to write prescriptions, but may not have their own forms for each hospital in which they work. For this purpose, the boards of medicine and pharmacy permit a <u>designated prescriber</u> at a facility that has <u>25 or more physicians</u> to order security prescription forms for their facility that <u>do not include</u> the <u>pre-printed prescriber information</u> (prescriber's name, category of licensure, license number, DEA number, and address of the prescribing practitioner).[179] These security forms will be signed out by the designated prescriber in a record book that includes the name to whom they were given, the category of license and number, the DEA number, and the quantity of security forms issued. The record must be kept in the health facility for <u>three years</u>.

**Exceptions to Using the California Security Form for the Terminally Ill**

A prescription for a controlled substance is exempt from using a security form if the prescriber has certified that the patient is terminally ill by writing the words "<u>11159.2 exemption</u>" on a plain prescription form. For this purpose, "terminally ill" means a patient who is suffering from an incurable/irreversible illness that is expected to cause death within <u>one year</u>. The controlled substance is used to help control pain and/or other symptoms associated with the terminal illness.

179   H&SC 11162.1(c)

## INSTITUTION STYLE SECURITY PRESCRIPTION FORM SAMPLE IN A MULTIPLE DRUG FORMAT

Institution forms can <u>only</u> be used by health care facilities licensed under Health & Safety Code section 1250. Generally, these are 24-hour acute care hospitals, skilled nursing facilities, etc. The forms are preprinted with the facility and the facility's "designated prescriber" information as indicated below. The actual prescriber information will be printed, handwritten, or stamped on the form when the prescription is written.

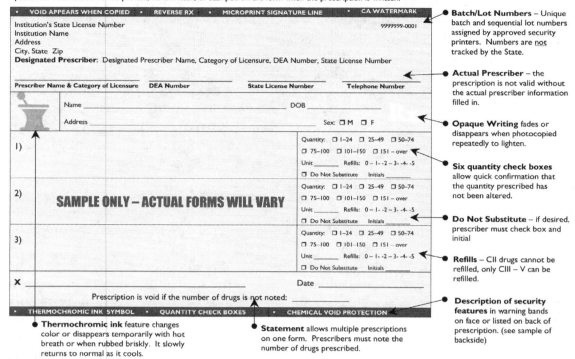

- **Batch/Lot Numbers** – Unique batch and sequential lot numbers assigned by approved security printers. Numbers are <u>not</u> tracked by the State.

- **Actual Prescriber** – the prescription is not valid without the actual prescriber information filled in.

- **Opaque Writing** fades or disappears when photocopied repeatedly to lighten.

- **Six quantity check boxes** allow quick confirmation that the quantity prescribed has not been altered.

- **Do Not Substitute** – if desired, prescriber must check box and initial

- **Refills** – CII drugs cannot be refilled, only CIII – V can be refilled.

- **Description of security features** in warning bands on face or listed on back of prescription. (see sample of backside)

- **Thermochromic ink** feature changes color or disappears temporarily with hot breath or when rubbed briskly. It slowly returns to normal as it cools.

- **Statement** allows multiple prescriptions on one form. Prescribers must note the number of drugs prescribed.

*Image courtesy of the California Board of Pharmacy*

## SAMPLE BACKSIDE OF SECURITY PRESCRIPTION FORM

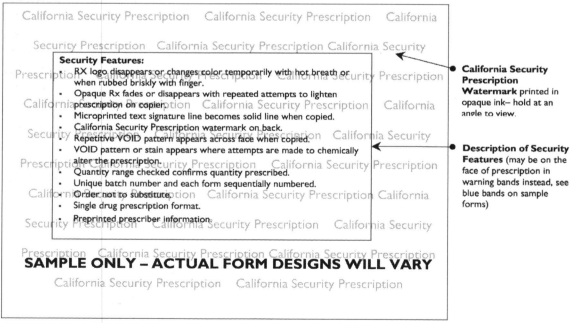

- **California Security Prescription Watermark** printed in opaque ink– hold at an angle to view.

- **Description of Security Features** (may be on the face of prescription in warning bands instead, see blue bands on sample forms)

*Image courtesy of the California Board of Pharmacy*

## Oral Prescriptions for Controlled Substances

Pharmacists can receive schedules III, IV, and V verbally (over the phone) if the pharmacist reduces the prescription to writing (writes the prescription on the pharmacy's paper prescription form) and includes all information required for a valid prescription (with the exception of the prescriber's signature and date).

Oral prescriptions for schedule II drugs are not valid unless they meet one of these two exceptions, in which case they can be taken over the phone, and reduced to writing by the pharmacist:

- In an emergency situation, the pharmacist can fill enough of a schedule II drug to tide the patient over until a valid prescription can be received. Oral, emergency prescriptions for schedule II drugs are discussed further in this manual under Emergency Filling.

- If the patient is a resident of a licensed skilled nursing facility, an intermediate care facility, a home health agency, or a hospice.[180]

## Faxed Prescriptions for Controlled Substances

Faxed prescriptions are acceptable for schedule III – V drugs as long all information required for a valid prescription is included and the prescriber manually signs the fax before sending it to the pharmacy. Prescribers should use a regular prescription form to write for schedule III – V drugs before faxing it to the pharmacy. If the prescriber uses a security form, the text "VOID" (written in thermochromic ink) can appear due to the heat emitted by the fax machine during transmission. This is acceptable to fill as long as the pharmacist validates the faxed prescription by contacting the prescriber's office for verification.[181]

Faxed prescriptions for schedule II drugs cannot serve as the original prescription. However, it is a common practice for a prescriber to provide a patient with a written prescription for a schedule II drug and to fax the same prescription to the pharmacy in order to alert the pharmacy that the patient is on the way. This will permit the pharmacy to fill the prescription as the patient is walking or driving over to the pharmacy. The pharmacist cannot dispense the schedule II drug to the patient until the patient hands in the written prescription to the pharmacy. The written prescription is then verified against the faxed prescription before dispensing.[182] It is not acceptable, even as an alert, for patients to fax prescriptions to a pharmacy.

The only time a faxed prescription for a schedule II drug is valid is if it is written for a patient of a licensed skilled nursing facility, an intermediate care facility, a home health agency or a hospice. The pharmacist will need to produce, sign, and date a hard copy of the prescription before filling it.[183]

180   H&SC 11167.5
181   http://www.pharmacy.ca.gov/licensees/prescribe_dispense.shtml (accessed 2017 Nov 1).
182   21 CFR 1306.11(a)
183   H&SC 11167.5

## Electronic Prescriptions for Controlled Substances

With the advancement of technology, most healthcare facilities are operating electronically — this includes electronic medical records, computer-based prescribing systems, and networks to transmit and receive prescriptions. When prescriptions are electronically transmitted entirely through software, safeguards must be in place to prevent unauthorized persons from hacking into the system and illegally transmitting controlled substance prescriptions. In 2010, the DEA released final rules that permit Electronic Prescriptions for Controlled Substances (EPCS) in schedules II – V.

The prescribers and pharmacies must use DEA-approved software to send and receive EPCS. The DEA requires a third party audit to review the software used by the prescriber and the pharmacy.

The credentials that are permitted for DEA-sanctioned validation will be two of the following factors:[184]

■ Something you know (such as a password or response to a question whose answer is known only to the practitioner)

■ Something you have (a hard token, which is a cryptographic key stored on a hardware device kept separately from the computer being accessed, such as a PDA, cell phone, smart card, or flash drive)

■ Something you are (biometric information, such as an iris or fingerprint scan)

Knowledge factors are easily observed, guessed, hacked and used without the practitioner's knowledge. This is why a hard token or biometric information must be used as well. Prescribers must use a two-factor authentication method to sign and transmit e-prescriptions. For example, the prescriber may enter a user name and password into the e-prescribing software. Before allowing the prescriber to sign, the e-prescribing software might send a text with an access code to the prescriber's cell phone. The prescriber would then enter the one-time use code from the text message. The password serves as one factor and the access code serves as the second factor. In order to compromise access, someone would need to have access to both the prescriber's user name and password and the prescriber's cell phone.

As an alternative to using two-factor authentication to sign the EPCS, the prescriber can use a digital certificate. A digital certificate contains the user's credentials and is issued by the DEA. Keep in mind that the prescriber's and the pharmacy's software used to transmit and receive the prescription must have the capability to transmit and verify the authentication factors or digital certificate. Electronic prescriptions for controlled substances are invalid if sent from software that is not yet DEA approved.

---

184   http://www.deadiversion.usdoj.gov/ecomm/e_rx/faq/practitioners.htm (accessed 2018 Feb 16).

## Multiple Prescriptions for Schedule II Drugs

Despite schedule II drugs having the most abuse potential out of all FDA-approved drugs, there is no federal or California regulation addressing the quantity limit for a single prescription of a schedule II drug. Nevertheless, prescribers are conservative in determining a day supply for schedule II prescriptions due to the rising deaths from drug abuse, and the awareness regarding appropriate use.

Some patients have a legitimate medical need (such as stimulants for ADHD or *Dilaudid* to treat cancer pain) for the long-term use of schedule II drugs. Since refills for schedule II drugs are prohibited and prescribers are usually conservative when authorizing a quantity for a single prescription, patients may need to visit the prescriber often to obtain a new prescription. This can cause unnecessary burden since the patient or caregiver may need to take time off from work for the doctor's appointment, determine transportation to and from the doctor's office, and pay an additional copay for each doctor's visit.

In 2007, the DEA provided a work-around for prescribers to issue multiple schedule II prescriptions for schedule II drugs in a single office visit. The prescriber can write for multiple (usually two or three) prescriptions for a schedule II drug which are filled sequentially, and cannot exceed a 90-day supply in total. The prescription cannot be post-dated. The prescriber must include two dates: when the prescription was written, and the earliest acceptable fill date. For example, if the patient was seen on April 1, 2018, the prescriber can provide the patient with three identical prescriptions, each for a 30-day supply of the schedule II drug, and all dated with the issue date of April 1, 2018. The first prescription can be filled on the day it was written (April 1, 2018), the second prescription will include the earliest possible fill date ("do not fill until May 1, 2018") and the third prescription will also include the earliest possible fill date ("do not fill until June 1, 2018"). The prescriber must indicate the "earliest acceptable fill date" in order to prevent the patient from filling more than one prescription at the same time at different pharmacies. This allows the patient to make less trips to the prescriber's office while still providing a mechanism for the prescriber to prevent drug diversion since the patient is only allowed to pick up a limited quantity at a time.

## Pre-signing and Post-dating Prescriptions for Controlled Substances

A prescription for a controlled substance must be dated and signed on the date when issued. Therefore, pre-dating and post-dating prescriptions are illegal.

Physicians had pre-dated (pre-signed) prescription blanks in the past to enable other healthcare providers (e.g., nurses) to issue prescriptions to patients while the physicians are out of the office. The physician would sign and date a prescription blank, while another healthcare provider would fill in the rest of the prescription at a later time with the patient's name, medication, and directions. Pre-signing prescription blanks is illegal and has resulted in disciplinary action and suspension of the prescriber's medical license. Pharmacists should not fill prescriptions that are suspected to be pre-signed.

As mentioned previously, postdating prescriptions is not allowed. If it is the prescriber's intention to issue multiple prescriptions to be filled sequentially, the prescriber must indicate two dates: when the prescription was written and the earliest fill date.

## Correcting Errors or Omissions on a Controlled Substance Prescription

All prescriptions for <u>controlled substances</u> must be <u>signed and dated by the prescriber</u>.[185] This information cannot be written in by the pharmacist or intern. Correcting errors or omissions for schedule II drugs are stricter. For schedule II drugs, the pharmacist cannot make any changes to the issue date, the prescriber's name, the prescriber's signature, the patient's name, or the drug's name. Minor misspellings can be revised at the pharmacist's discretion. The pharmacist or intern can make changes to any other information on the prescription as long as the pharmacist <u>verifies the change</u> with the prescriber first.

## Prescriptions from Out-of-State

Pharmacists may dispense written and oral prescriptions from out-of-state prescribers, with certain requirements and exceptions for controlled substances.

A prescription for a controlled substance (schedule <u>II, III, IV, and V</u>) issued by an out-of-state prescriber can be filled and <u>delivered</u> (mailed) to the patient by a California pharmacy, if the prescription <u>meets the requirements</u> for controlled substance prescriptions of the <u>state it was written in</u>.[186] The prescriber must be registered with the DEA. This is to accommodate patients who use out-of-state mail order pharmacies to fill prescriptions.

California pharmacies may dispense prescriptions for Schedule <u>III, IV, and V</u> drugs written from out-of-state prescribers <u>directly</u> to the patient if the prescription <u>meets the requirements</u> for controlled substance prescriptions of the <u>state it was written in</u>.[187] A prescriber writing for scheduled drugs must be registered with the DEA. This means that the patient can walk into a California pharmacy, drop off the prescription written by an out-of-state prescriber on a correct form, come back to the pharmacy once the prescription is filled, and pick up the filled prescription from the California pharmacy. California pharmacies may not dispense prescriptions written for <u>schedule II drugs</u> written from out-of-state prescribers directly to the patient.

## THE PRESCRIBER'S AND PHARMACIST'S CORRESPONDING RESPONSIBILITY

Pharmacists are the last line of defense in preventing controlled substances from getting into the wrong hands. A drug can be scheduled due to risks of addiction, physical dependence, and accidental or intentional drug diversion. Diversion is defined as drugs going to other individuals than for whom it was originally intended for.

185   H&SC 11164(a)(1)
186   H&SC 11164.1(a)(1)
187   H&SC 11164.1(b)

A practitioner can issue valid prescriptions for a legitimate medical purpose only. The condition being treated must be one that the prescriber would be expected to treat. If the pharmacist does not believe that the prescription is for a legitimate medical need, then the pharmacist has the right not to fill it. Any concerns regarding the prescription should be investigated. Both the prescriber and the pharmacist share responsibility to prevent drug diversion.[188]

## Recognizing Red Flags to Prevent Drug Diversion

More Americans die from prescription drug abuse than from using street drugs such as heroin and crack cocaine. As part of their professional practice, pharmacists must do their best to prevent prescription drug abuse and diversion. If appropriate, the pharmacist has the right and obligation to tell the patient, "I do not feel comfortable filling this prescription," or "I will not fill this prescription." It is considered a felony offense for a pharmacist to knowingly fill an invalid or fraudulent prescription. The law does not require a pharmacist to dispense a prescription of suspicious origin or containing one or more of the following red flags:

- Irregularities on the face of the prescription itself

- Nervous patient demeanor

- Age or presentation of patient (e.g., youthful patients seeking chronic pain medications)

- Multiple patients all with the same residential address

- Multiple prescribers for the same patient for duplicate therapy

- Cash payments

- Frequent requests for early refills

- Suspicious prescriptions brought in at the busiest time while the patient decides to wait for it to be filled

- Prescriptions written for an unusually large quantity of drugs

- Prescriptions written for duplicative drug therapy

- Initial prescriptions written for strong opiates

- Long distances traveled from the patient's home to the prescriber's office or to the pharmacy

- Irregularities in the prescriber's qualifications in relation to the type of medication/s prescribed

188   H&SC 11153

- Prescriptions that are written outside of the prescriber's medical specialty

- Prescriptions for medications with no logical connection to an illness or condition

- Patients coming to the pharmacy in groups (especially if most of the patients live far away from the pharmacy or prescriber and each patient has similar prescriptions issued by the same prescriber)

- The same diagnosis codes for many patients

- The same combinations of drugs prescribed for multiple patients

### Controlled Substance Utilization Review and Evaluation System

The Controlled Substance Utilization Review and Evaluation System (CURES) is California's Prescription Drug Monitoring Program (PDMP), which is a database of all prescriptions dispensed for schedules II – IV drugs. Prescribers and pharmacists can quickly review a patient's scheduled prescriptions by accessing the database online and printing out a patient activity report. These are used whenever drug abuse or diversion is suspected. The report lists the scheduled prescriptions the patient received, the prescribers, the pharmacies that filled them, and other dispensing information. Each pharmacy submits dispensing data for schedule II – IV drugs to CURES on a weekly basis.[189] All California pharmacists with active licenses must be registered to access CURES.[190]

A healthcare practitioner must review a patient's controlled substance history from the CURES database no earlier than 24 hours, or the previous business day, before he or she prescribes, orders, administers, or furnishes a schedule II – IV drug to the patient for the first time and once every four months if the controlled drug is still being used.[191] There are some exemptions.

## REFILLS OF CONTROLLED SUBSTANCES

### Controlled Substances Eligible for Refills

Schedule V drugs can be refilled up to 6 months from the date of issue. There is no refill or day supply limit as long as it is authorized by the prescriber.[192]

Schedules III and IV prescriptions may be refilled up to 5 times within 6 months of the date written, and all refills taken together cannot exceed a 120-day supply.[193] The original fill does not count as a "refill" towards the 120-day supply limit. For example, if the prescription for a schedule III drug is written as "Take 1 tablet by mouth daily, #30 tablets, 5 refills" and the patient takes the drug every day, then the maximum refills the patient can have is 120 tablets (for a 120-day supply, not counting the original fill), which is reached at 4 refills.

189   H&SC 11165(d)
190   H&SC 11165.1(a)(1)(A)(ii)
191   H&SC 11165.4(a)(2)
192   H&SC 11166
193   H&SC 11200

A pharmacy may use only one of the two systems described below (paper or electronic) for storage and retrieval of prescription order refill information of schedule III – IV controlled substances:

- Paper recordkeeping system:

  - For each refill dispensed, the pharmacist must notate on the back of the prescription: his or her initials, the date dispensed, and the amount dispensed. If the amount dispensed is not notated for each refill, it is assumed that the pharmacist dispensed a refill for the full refill amount.

- Electronic recordkeeping system (either method described is acceptable):

  - A daily, hard copy printout of refills for controlled substances with the <u>signature</u> and <u>date</u> of <u>all the pharmacists</u> involved with the dispensing. This signifies that the pharmacists agree that the printout is correct and that is what they refilled for the day. The printout must be provided to the pharmacy within <u>72 hours</u> of the date on which the refill was dispensed.

  - A bound logbook or separate file documenting each day's refills. Each dispensing pharmacist during the shift signs a statement saying that what they dispensed is correctly listed in the logbook or file.

Refills on schedule II prescriptions are prohibited.


## PARTIAL FILLING OF CONTROLLED SUBSTANCES
Partial filling can <u>decrease the amount of unnecessary, unwanted, and unused prescription medications</u>. For example: a patient with a tooth extraction can receive a partial fill of drugs, and can pick up the remaining amount available if necessary.


### Partial Fills of Schedule III – V Prescriptions
Partial fills for refills of schedule III, IV, and V controlled substances are permitted if it is recorded in the same manner as a refill and if the total quantity dispensed in all of the fills does not exceed the total quantity prescribed. No dispensing can occur beyond <u>6 months</u> from the date of issue. Partial fills are <u>not considered refills</u>. For example, a patient is prescribed *Ultram* #60, with two refills. This is equivalent to 180 tablets to be dispensed over a 6-month period from the date of issue. Theoretically, the patient could come into the pharmacy every day for 90 days and receive two tablets. This would not be preferable to the pharmacy, and is an extreme example. It is used to demonstrate that the law is broad on the filling of partial refills, which may be required by a patient due to the cost of the drug.

## Partial Fills of Schedule II Prescriptions

Partial filling of schedule II prescriptions is permissible if:

| SCENARIO | DEADLINE FOR REMAINING BALANCE TO BE FILLED |
|---|---|
| The pharmacy does not have sufficient stock of the drug[194] | 72 hours |
| Partial filling of an emergency oral prescription[195] | 72 hours |
| The partial fill is requested by the patient or the practitioner that wrote the prescription[196] | 30 days |
| Partial filling for terminally ill patients[197] | 60 days |
| Partial filling for LTCF residents[198] | 60 days |

The total quantity dispensed in all partial fillings cannot exceed the total quantity prescribed. When a pharmacist fills less than the full amount on the prescription, he or she notes on the prescription the amount filled. The remaining balance must be filled by a certain time, or else the remaining balance is forfeited.

It is common for pharmacies to partially fill controlled substance prescriptions for terminally ill patients or SNF residents in order to reduces drug diversion and waste that can occur if the patient expires before the medications are finished. The term "terminally ill" is often used in hospice settings to indicate that the patient is expected to have less than 12 months to live. These prescriptions are often written for schedule II opioids, which are used to relieve severe pain during the patient's remaining days. The reason for the partial fill must be noted on the prescription, such as "terminally ill" or "SNF resident." For terminally ill patients or SNF residents, the pharmacist can partially fill prescriptions in increments for up to 60 days from the date the prescription was written.

## EMERGENCY FILLING OF CONTROLLED SUBSTANCES

### Emergency Filling of Schedule III – V Drugs without Prescriber's Authorization

As discussed in the Pharmacy Practice section, emergency refills without the prescriber's authorization is allowed for non-scheduled and schedules III – V drugs if the prescriber is unavailable to authorize the refill and, if in the pharmacist's professional judgment, failure to refill the prescription might interrupt the patient's ongoing care and have a significant adverse effect on the patient's well-being. The pharmacist must make every reasonable effort to contact the prescriber.

---

194  CCR 1745 (a)
195  21 USC §829(f)(2)(B)
196  B&PC 4052.10 (effective July 1, 2018)
197  CCR 1745 (a-c)
198  same as above

## Emergency Filling of Schedule II Drugs

In most circumstances, prescribers cannot call in prescriptions for schedule II drugs; these must be authorized as a written or electronic prescription. However, the DEA permits emergency dispensing of orally authorized prescriptions for schedule II drugs if the immediate administration of the drug is necessary to avoid patient harm and if there is no reasonable alternative. Electronic prescriptions provide an immediate method to transmit an original prescription to the pharmacy, but a verbally authorized prescription can still be needed if the prescriber's or pharmacy's EPCS system experiences downtime.

If the pharmacist is not familiar with the prescriber, he or she must make a reasonable effort to determine that the oral authorization came from a DEA registered practitioner, which can include a call back to the prescribing individual practitioner using the telephone number listed in a public directory and/or other good faith efforts to insure the prescriber's identity. The prescription must be reduced to writing immediately by the pharmacist and must contain all the necessary information, except for the prescriber signature. The quantity dispensed should be the minimum necessary amount until a prescription can be written or electronically transmitted. This amount is up to the pharmacist's professional judgment.

The prescriber must provide an original prescription (written or electronic) by the 7th day following the fill date. The written prescription can be hand-delivered or mailed and postmarked by the 7th day. The written prescription needs to include the statement "Authorization for Emergency Dispensing" on the face and the date of the oral prescription. Once received, the pharmacist must attach the written prescription to the emergency oral prescription. For electronic prescriptions, the pharmacist must annotate the record of the electronic prescription with the emergency authorization and date of the oral order. If the original prescription is not received, the pharmacist must report to the California Bureau of Narcotic Enforcement within 144 hours and must also report to the DEA.[199, 200]

## FEDERAL WARNING LABEL FOR CONTROLLED SUBSTANCES

Schedule II, III and IV drugs are required to have the following warning on the container when dispensed: *"CAUTION: Federal law prohibits the transfer of this drug to any person other than the person for whom it was prescribed."* Schedule V drugs are not required to have the above statement affixed to the label.[201]

## TRANSFERRING CONTROLLED SUBSTANCES PRESCRIPTIONS

Prescriptions for schedule III, IV and V drugs are only allowed one transfer that must be by direct communication between two licensed pharmacists. The only exception is if the pharmacies share a "real-time, online database of the patients" (such as pharmacy stores in the same pharmacy chain). With this type of shared prescription database, pharmacies may transfer up to the maximum refills permitted by law and by the prescriber's authorization.

199   H&SC 11167(d)
200   https://www.deadiversion.usdoj.gov/21cfr/cfr/1306/1306_11.htm (accessed 2018 Feb 16).
201   21 CFR 290.5

For the transferring pharmacy, the prescription hard copy is pulled and "void" is written on the face of the prescription. For the receiving pharmacy, the prescription is reduced to writing by the pharmacist and "transfer" is written on the face of the transferred prescription.

The DEA number of each pharmacy must be recorded and all other information is recorded as required (See Pharmacy Practice, Prescription Transfers). Alternatively, the above information may be documented electronically. Records must be kept for three years.

Schedule II prescriptions cannot be transferred.

## DELIVERING CONTROLLED SUBSTANCES TO PATIENTS

United States Postal Services regulations permit pharmacies to deliver controlled substances to patients.[202]

The following preparation and packaging standards must be met:

*It is permissible according to federal law to mail scheduled and non-scheduled drugs; the outer packaging cannot indicate the contents.*

- The prescription is placed in a plain outer container or securely wrapped in plain paper.

- The prescription label contains the name and address of the pharmacy, practitioner, or other person dispensing the prescription.

## PATIENT IDENTIFICATION BEFORE DISPENSING CONTROLLED SUBSTANCES

If a prescription for a controlled substance is orally or electronically transmitted, the patient or the patient's representative must provide proof of identify if he or she is unknown to the pharmacy staff.[203]

## TREATMENT OF DRUG ADDICTION

The National Institute on Drug Abuse defines addiction as a chronic, relapsing brain disease that is characterized by compulsive drug seeking and use, despite harmful consequences. Simply stated, it is a strong need to use drugs for a recreational/emotional purpose.

The rising death toll due to inappropriate/excessive opioid use has spurred a national movement to make naloxone more widely available to the public. Naloxone is an opioid antagonist that binds to and displaces the opioid from the receptor sites. Pharmacists can furnish naloxone to patients. See the Furnishing Naloxone discussion in this manual.

---

202   *Publication 52, Hazardous, Restricted, and Perishable Mail, § 453.4*
203   *B&PC 4075*

## Opioid Treatment Programs

It is estimated that ~ 1 million people in the United States are addicted to heroin and other opioids, including prescription drugs such as oxycodone, hydromorphone and hydrocodone.[204] Patients with this type of addiction are more likely to be co-infected with HIV, hepatitis and sexually transmitted infections. Mental health problems are common among patients with addiction. Criminal histories often stem from the addiction. Treating addiction saves lives, helps families, and reduces healthcare costs.

Historically, prescribing controlled substances to treat opioid dependence was only allowed in opioid treatment programs.[205] Opioid treatment programs must register with the Drug Enforcement Administration with DEA Form 363. Methadone is an effective schedule II drug used by opioid treatment clinics to treat opioid dependence. The 40 mg dose is only indicated for opioid addiction; the lower doses are indicated for pain and opioid addiction. To prevent drug diversion, patients must visit the clinic every day for a minimum of three months to receive and ingest a supervised dose of methadone. After three months, eligible patients can gradually take home increased amounts of doses. This created a great barrier for treatment, especially for patients living in rural areas.

## Opioid Dependence Treatment in an Office-Based Setting

The ability for patients to obtain treatment for opioid addiction improved when the Drug Addiction Treatment Act (DATA) of 2000 was passed. DATA 2000 permits physicians to prescribe and dispense schedule III – V drugs to treat opioid addiction outside of a opioid treatment clinic. Patients no longer had to make a daily trip to the clinic for a supervised dose, and instead could receive a prescription to be filled at a pharmacy. Only drugs indicated for opioid dependence (e.g., *Suboxone, Subutex, Probuphine*) can be used. The Comprehensive Addiction and Recovery Act (CARA) was passed in year 2016, allowing qualified nurse practitioner and physician assistants to treat narcotic dependence as well. These practitioners do not need to register as an opioid treatment program.

DATA 2000 requires practitioner training. Once this is completed, the practitioner is referred to as a "DATA waived practitioner" and is given a DATA 2000 waiver unique identification number (UIN). The number is the same as their original DEA number except that the letter "X" replaces the first letter. For example, if Dr. Wendy Clark's DEA number is AC2143799, her UIN would be XC2143799. The UIN is in addition to a prescriber's DEA number and both numbers should be on prescriptions. Pharmacists can also verify a prescriber's DATA waiver online.[206] DATA waived practitioners can treat up to 30 patients at any one time for the first year. After the first year, they can request to increase the limit to treating 100 patients at any one time. Practitioners who have held a 100-patient buprenorphine waiver for at least one year can be eligible to apply for a 275-patient waiver by holding additional credentialing or by practicing in a qualified practice setting.

204   http://www.cdc.gov/drugoverdose/pdf/hhs_prescription_drug_abuse_report_09.2013.pdf (accessed 2018 Jan 26).
205   42 CFR § 8.12
206   https://www.samhsa.gov/bupe/lookup-form (accessed 2018 Jan 17).

A practitioner without a DATA waiver can administer (but not prescribe) a day's worth of treatment at one time to a patient while the proper referral to an opioid treatment program is being arranged. This can be done for up to 3 days.

## Pharmacist Recovery Program for Substance Abuse and Mental Illness

Substance abuse can happen to anyone. A recent study indicated that 46% of the pharmacists and 62% of the pharmacy interns admitted to using controlled substances at some time without a valid prescription. The pharmacists' greater access to drugs increases the risk for substance abuse. The board contracts with Maximus, Inc. to provide confidential assessment, referral, and monitoring services for the Pharmacists Recovery Program.[207] The purpose of the program is to evaluate the drug abuse and/or mental illness, develop a treatment plan, monitor progress and provide support. The individual receives the help to recover and, if possible, return to practicing pharmacy.

The Pharmacy Recovery Program accepts referrals on a _voluntary basis_. Any pharmacist or intern in California who is experiencing alcohol or other drug abuse or mental illness can voluntarily seek assistance by contacting a 24-hour toll-free number. All voluntary requests for information and assistance are strictly confidential; this information is not subject to discovery or subpoena. Family, friends, employers, and professional colleagues are also encouraged to contact the program for information and assistance.

The pharmacy must have a procedure in place for when a licensed pharmacy staff member is found to be chemically, mentally, or physically impaired to the extent it affects his or her ability to practice, or is found to have engaged in the theft, diversion, or self-use of drugs. If a pharmacist suspects another pharmacist is impaired at work, they must report this to the board within _14 days_.

The board also uses the program for pharmacists who are chemically dependent or mentally impaired. The board may _refer a pharmacist to the recovery program in lieu of discipline_ if there has been no other significant violation of the pharmacy law. In cases that involve a serious violation, the board may refer a pharmacist to the program in addition to discipline.

## DISTRIBUTION OF CONTROLLED SUBSTANCES BETWEEN DEA REGISTRANTS

A Form 222, or its electronic equivalent, must be used to distribute schedule I and II drugs. An invoice is used to distribute schedule III, IV, and V drugs, which must contain the following information: drug name, dosage form, strength, quantity, date transferred, and recipient's information (name, address, DEA registration number). All records of these transfers (Form 222, invoice, inventory records) are kept for at least _three years_.

---

207   http://www.pharmacy.ca.gov/licensees/personal/pharmacist_recovery.shtml (accessed 2018 Feb 16).

## Pharmacy Going out of Business

If a pharmacy goes out of business or is acquired by a new pharmacy, it can transfer the controlled substances to another pharmacy. A complete inventory must be taken that will be used as the final inventory of the registrant who is going out of business. It is also used as the initial inventory for the registrant acquiring the controlled substances. A copy of the inventory must be included in the records of each pharmacy. Inventory records are not sent to the DEA. Inventories are taken at either the opening or closing of the business day, and the time taken (opening or closing) must be recorded on the inventory.

A pharmacy can also transfer controlled substances to the original supplier, manufacturer, or distributor for disposal.

## Selling Controlled Substances

A pharmacy can sell controlled substances to other pharmacies or prescribers (without being registered as a distributor) as long as the total number of dosage units does not exceed 5% of the total number of controlled substances dosage units dispensed per calendar year. If the total sold exceeds 5%, the pharmacy must register with the DEA as a wholesaler. Both parties must be registered with the DEA to dispense controlled substances. If a pharmacy is selling schedule II drugs, a Form 222 must be used. The pharmacy selling the schedule II drugs is responsible for forwarding Copy 2 of the Form 222 to the DEA by the end of the month.

A healthcare practitioner cannot write a prescription to get controlled substances for the purpose of stocking them for "office use" or to dispense directly to patients. The practitioner would need to purchase the controlled substances from the pharmacy or wholesaler.

## REPORTING THE LOSS OR THEFT OF CONTROLLED SUBSTANCES

Losing a significant quantity of controlled substances is a erious issue in terms of drug diversion, corresponding responsibility, and cost to the pharmacy.

Pharmacies must report <u>significant</u> losses and all thefts of controlled substances to the local DEA office in writing within <u>one business day</u> upon discovery and complete a <u>DEA 106</u> when <u>circumstances</u> of the theft or significant loss are known.[208] The initial notice to the DEA can be done by faxing or mailing a short statement to the local DEA office. The DEA Form 106 does not need to be submitted immediately since the pharmacy may need more time to investigate what happened. If it is subsequently determined that no theft or significant loss occurred, then the DEA Form 106 does not need to be submitted at all, but the DEA should also be notified.[209]

Pharmacists must also report <u>all</u> controlled substance drug losses to the California Board of Pharmacy within <u>14 calendar days</u> for losses due to licensed employee theft[210], or <u>30 calendar days</u> for any other type of loss.[211] A copy of the DEA Form 106 can be sent to the Board of Pharmacy. However, notifications of drug losses sent to the Board of Pharmacy may be in any format as long as it includes the necessary information.[212]

The following considerations are used to determine if the loss is significant:

■ If the drugs could be subject to diversion

■ The specific substances lost or stolen The quantity lost in relation to the type of business

■ The individuals with access to the lost or stolen drug

■ History or pattern of losses or local diversion issues


Any unique circumstances surrounding the loss or theft

208  21 CFR 1301.74(c)
209  https://www.deadiversion.usdoj.gov/fed_regs/rules/2003/fr0708.htm (accessed 2018 Feb 16).
210  B&PC 4104
211  CCR 1715.6
212  http://www.pharmacy.ca.gov/licensees/facility/dea106.shtml (accessed 2018 Feb 16).

## REPORT OF THEFT OR LOSS OF CONTROLLED SUBSTANCES

Federal Regulations require registrants to submit a detailed report of any theft or loss of Controlled Substances to the Drug Enforcement Administration.

Complete the front and back of this form in triplicate. Forward the original and duplicate copies to the nearest DEA Office. Retain the triplicate copy for your records. Some states may also require a copy of this report.

OMB APPROVAL
No. 1117-0001

**1. Name and Address of Registrant (include ZIP Code)**

ZIP CODE

**2. Phone No. (Include Area Code)**

**3. DEA Registration Number**

2 ltr. prefix          7 digit suffix

**4. Date of Theft or Loss**

**5. Principal Business of Registrant (Check one)**

| | | | |
|---|---|---|---|
| 1 ☐ Pharmacy | | 5 ☐ Distributor |
| 2 ☐ Practitioner | | 6 ☐ Methadone Program |
| 3 ☐ Manufacturer | | 7 ☐ Other (Specify) |
| 4 ☐ Hospital/Clinic | | |

**6. County in which Registrant is located**

**7. Was Theft reported to Police?**
☐ Yes   ☐ No

**8. Name and Telephone Number of Police Department (Include Area Code)**

**9. Number of Thefts or Losses Registrant has experienced in the past 24 months**

**10. Type of Theft or Loss (Check one and complete items below as appropriate)**

| | | | | | |
|---|---|---|---|---|---|
| 1 ☐ Night break-in | 3 ☐ Employee pilferage | 5 ☐ Other (Explain) |
| 2 ☐ Armed robbery | 4 ☐ Customer theft | 6 ☐ Lost in transit (Complete Item 14) |

**11. If Armed Robbery, was anyone:**

Killed? ☐ No   ☐ Yes (How many) _____

Injured? ☐ No   ☐ Yes (How many) _____

**12. Purchase value to registrant of Controlled Substances taken?**

$

**13. Were any pharmaceuticals or merchandise taken?**
☐ No   ☐ Yes (Est. Value)

$

**14. IF LOST IN TRANSIT, COMPLETE THE FOLLOWING:**

**A. Name of Common Carrier**

**B. Name of Consignee**

**C. Consignee's DEA Registration Number**

**D. Was the carton received by the customer?**
☐ Yes   ☐ No

**E. If received, did it appear to be tampered with?**
☐ Yes   ☐ No

**F. Have you experienced losses in transit from this same carrier in the past?**
☐ No   ☐ Yes (How Many) _____

**15. What identifying marks, symbols, or price codes were on the labels of these containers that would assist in identifying the products?**

**16. If Official Controlled Substance Order Forms (DEA-222) were stolen, give numbers.**

**17. What security measures have been taken to prevent future thefts or losses?**

### PRIVACY ACT INFORMATION

AUTHORITY: Section 301 of the Controlled Substances Act of 1970 (PL 91-513).
PURPOSE: Report theft or loss of Controlled Substances.
ROUTINE USES: The Controlled Substances Act authorizes the production of special reports required for statistical and analytical purposes. Disclosures of information from this system are made to the following categories of users for the purposes stated:

  A. Other Federal law enforcement and regulatory agencies for law enforcement and regulatory purposes.
  B. State and local law enforcement and regulatory agencies for law enforcement and regulatory purposes.

EFFECT: Failure to report theft or loss of controlled substances may result in penalties under Section 402 and 403 of the Controlled Substances Act.

In accordance with the Paperwork Reduction Act of 1995, no person is required to respond to a collection of information unless it displays a ly valid OMB control number. The valid OMB control number for this collection of information is 1117-0001. Public reporting burden for this collection of information is estimated to average 30 minutes per response, including the time for reviewing instructions, searching existing data sources, gathering and maintaining the data needed, and completing and reviewing the collection of information.

FORM DEA - 106 (11-00) Previous editions obsolete

**CONTINUE ON REVERSE**

Image courtesy of the Drug Enforcement Administration

## DISPENSING AID-IN-DYING DRUGS

California's End of Life Option Act is effective as of June 9, 2016. The end of life option can be referred to as death with dignity or physician-assisted suicide. The act permits mentally competent, terminally-ill adults to receive and voluntarily self-administer drug/s to end their life in a peaceful, humane manner in a place and time of their choosing. Patients who wish to receive an aid-in-dying drug must be:

- 18+ years

- A California resident

- Mentally competent (capable of making and communicating healthcare decisions for him/herself)

- Diagnosed with a terminal illness that will lead to death within 6 months (confirmed by two physicians)

Procedure to receive and use the medication:

1.  The patient makes the first oral request to the physician. Patients who do not speak English can use a language interpreter. The physician must discuss the request for medication with the patient (and their interpreter, if applicable) alone to ensure that the request is voluntary.

2.  After at least 15 days from the initial oral request, the patient makes a second oral request to the physician.

3.  Anytime after the first oral request, a written request is given to the physician (the patient does not need to wait until after the second oral request to make the written request).

4.  After the physician receives all 3 requests, the physician can furnish the drugs directly to the patient or send a prescription directly to a pharmacist. If the physician is sending a prescription to a pharmacy, the physician must contact a pharmacist first and inform the pharmacist of the prescription for aid-in-dying drugs. The physician must then personally hand-deliver, mail, or electronically send the written prescription to the pharmacist. The patient is never in possession of the prescription.

5.  The patient picks up the medication from the pharmacy or has it delivered.

6.  The patient can change his/her mind about taking the medication at any time.

7.  The patient must complete the final attestation form (to be given to the attending physician) within 48 hours before taking the medication.

The schedule II controlled substances <u>secobarbital</u> and <u>pentobarbital</u> are likely drugs to be used for this purpose. The patient should be counseled on the importance of keeping the drug secure and out of the reach of children and pets. An anti-emetic should be taken an hour before the drug is taken. Secobarbital comes in capsules and pentobarbital comes in solution. If the contents of the capsules are opened, the drug can be mixed with juice to mask the bitter taste. A person (such as a relative or caregiver) who has unused drug after the death of the patient must properly dispose of it using the nearest DEA-registered collection receptacle, a law-enforcement sponsored take back event, or by any other lawful means (see the Patients Disposing Drugs section in this manual).

Death with dignity is a controversial issue as it goes against many healthcare providers' oath to do no harm. Pharmacists are not required to participate. A pharmacist can choose not to furnish the drugs due to conscientious, moral, or ethical objection.[213]

## NONPRESCRIPTION PRODUCTS WITH RESTRICTED SALES

### Pseudoephedrine, Ephedrine, Phenylpropanolamine, and Norpseudoephedrine

<u>Pseudoephedrine</u>, <u>ephedrine</u>, phenylpropanolamine, and norpseudoephedrine-containing products have restricted distribution because they can be used to make illicit drugs, including methamphetamine and amphetamine. The Combat Methamphetamine Epidemic Act of 2005 and state law applies to all four products, but one of them is not available in the U.S., and the other is for veterinary use (by prescription only); thus, the requirements are used primarily to control the sales of pseudoephedrine. This is the popular decongestant that is available as the branded drug *Sudafed* and comes in many non-branded single and combination cold products.

| DRUG | NOTES |
|------|-------|
| Pseudoephedrine (e.g., *Sudafed*) | In many cough and cold products |
| Ephedrine (*Bronkaid, Primatene*) | Asthma products |
| Norpseudoephedrine (e.g., *Eatless, Nobese*) | Not available in the U.S. |
| Phenylpropanolamine | By prescription only, for veterinary use |

The sale of these products must be <u>documented</u> and are subject to <u>quantity limits</u>. These products must be kept <u>behind the counter</u> or in a <u>locked cabinet</u>. They often are, but do not need to be, located in the pharmacy as long as the area with the products and logbook can be locked. The only exception to these requirements is the purchase of a single dose package of pseudoephedrine that contains a maximum of 60 mg (two of the 30 mg tablets). This exception does not apply to the other products.

213   *B&PC 733(b)(3)*

Over-the-counter purchases of these drugs are limited to a maximum of:

■ 3.6 grams per day

■ 9 grams in a 30-day period, or 7.5 grams in a 30-day period (mail order)

■ 3 packages per transaction[214]

The customer must show photo identification issued by the state/federal government (e.g., driver's license, state identification card, passport) or another acceptable form of identification[215]. The customers must record their name, address, and the date and time of the sale and sign the logbook. The store staff then must verify that the photo on the ID matches the customer and that the date and time are correct. Many pharmacies can swipe the driver's license to automatically record the name and address. The store staff must document the drug product and quantity the customer purchased.

The DEA requires that the logbook be kept for at least 2 years. It must be kept secured and the information in it cannot be shared with the public. Inspectors and law enforcement can have access to the logbook.

All pharmacies that sell these products must "self-certify" to the Attorney General of the US that they are trained in the regulations of selling pseudoephedrine, ephedrine, and phenyl-propanolamine.

### Hypodermic Needle and Syringe

A pharmacist can furnish hypodermic needles and syringes to patients without a prescription in the following situations:[216]

■ The pharmacist knows the patient and the pharmacist has previously been provided with a prescription or other proof of legitimate medical need for the needles and syringes (e.g., administering insulin).

■ To a person 18 years of age or older as a public health measure to prevent the transmission of HIV, viral hepatitis, and other bloodborne diseases among persons who use syringes and hypodermic needles, and to prevent subsequent infection of sexual partners, newborn children, or other persons. There is no limit on the number of needles and syringes that can be provided.

■ Use on animals, as long as the animal's owner is known to the pharmacist or the person's identity can be properly established.

■ For industrial use, as determined by the board.

---

214   H&SC 11100 (g)(3)
215   https://www.deadiversion.usdoj.gov/meth/alternate_ID2.pdf (accessed 2018 Feb 16).
216   B&PC 4145.5

Pharmacies that sell syringes without a prescription must:

- Store needles and syringes in a manner that ensures that they are not accessible to unauthorized persons.

- Provide for the safe disposal of needles and syringes by choosing one or more of the following options: selling or furnishing sharps containers or mail-back sharps containers, and/or providing on-site sharps collection and disposal. Pharmacies can take back used syringes only if enclosed in a sharps container.

- Provide written information or verbal counseling to customers at the time of sale on how to access drug treatment, access testing and treatment for HIV and HCV, and information about how to safely dispose of sharps waste.

## Dextromethorphan

Dextromethorphan is an over-the-counter (OTC) cough suppressant commonly found in more than 120 OTC cold medications, either alone (e.g., in the branded product *Delsym*), or in combination with other drugs. Dextromethorphan is often abused by teenagers for its euphoric effects. In high enough concentrations, dextromethorphan can cause visual and auditory hallucinations. Illicit use of dextromethorphan can be referred to as "Robo-tripping" or "skittling." Dextromethorphan is not currently scheduled under the Controlled Substances Act. Dextromethorphan-containing products cannot be sold to anyone under 18 years old without a prescription in California. The purchaser must provide a government-issued identification (with name, date of birth, description, and picture of the purchaser), unless the pharmacy staff reasonably assumes that the purchaser looks at least 25 years old. This practice will help avoid selling the product to those less than 18 years old.[217] Dextromethorphan products can be kept on the floor shelves outside of the pharmacy area with other OTC products, and the cashier staff can check for the age requirement.

---

*217  H&SC 11110*

# 4

# Pharmacy Operations

## FACILITY AND EQUIPMENT REQUIREMENTS

The board has certain requirements for the pharmacy practice site. The pharmacy must meet the following requirements:

- An unobstructed area of sufficient size for the safe practice of pharmacy.

- A sink with hot and cold running water.

- A readily accessible restroom.

- A suitable area for confidential patient consultation.

- Safeguards in place to prevent the theft of drugs and devices.

- The pharmacy premises, fixtures, and equipment are maintained in a clean and orderly condition, properly lighted and free from rodents and insects.

- The original board-issued pharmacy license and the current renewal are posted where they can be clearly read by the public.[218]

There are additional requirements if the pharmacy compounds sterile drugs:

- The pharmacy maintains written documentation regarding the facilities and equipment necessary for safe and accurate compounding, including records of certification of facilities or equipment, if applicable.

- All equipment used to compound drug products is stored, used and maintained in accordance with manufacturers' specifications.

- All equipment used to compound drug products is calibrated before use to ensure accuracy.

- Documentation of each calibration is recorded in writing and kept in the pharmacy.

218   B&PC 4058

## POLICIES AND PROCEDURES

A policy is a course of action for a specific activity or procedure. For example, the pharmacy's Quality Assurance P&P would outline the steps involved in conducting a quality assessment in order to reduce a type of medication error. P&P's help keep the pharmacy running efficiently. Each team member can use the P&P's to determine what should occur in various circumstances. The P&Ps are kept in the P&P manual. Having the manual and using it can protect the pharmacy in case of litigation.

Pharmacies must have the following P&Ps in place:

- Action to be taken to protect the public when a licensed individual employed by or with the pharmacy is known to be <u>chemically, mentally, or physically impaired</u> to the extent that it affects his or her ability to practice the profession or occupation authorized by his or her license, including the reporting to the board within <u>14 days</u>.[219]

- Action to be taken to protect the public when a licensed individual employed by or with the pharmacy is known to have engaged in the <u>theft</u> or <u>diversion</u> or <u>self-use of prescription drugs belonging to the pharmacy</u>, including the reporting to the board within <u>14 days</u>.[220]

- Oral consultation for discharge medications to an inpatient of a healthcare facility, or to an inmate of an adult correctional facility or juvenile detention facility.[221]

- Operation of the pharmacy during the temporary absence of the pharmacist for breaks and meal periods including authorized duties of personnel, pharmacist's responsibilities for checking all work performed by ancillary staff, and pharmacist's responsibility for maintaining the security of the pharmacy.[222]

- Assuring confidentiality of medical information if your pharmacy maintains the required dispensing information for prescriptions, other than controlled substances, in a shared common electronic file.[223]

- The delivery of drugs and devices to a secure storage facility, if the pharmacy accepts deliveries when the pharmacy is closed and there is no pharmacist present.[224]

- Compliance with the federal Combat Methamphetamine Epidemic Act of 2005.

- Reporting requirements to protect the public.[225]

- A policy to establish how a patient will receive a medication when a pharmacist has a conscientious objection.[226]

219  B&PC 4104(a), (c)
220  B&PC 4104(b), (c)
221  B&PC 4074, CCR 1707.2(b)(3)
222  CCR 1714.1(f)
223  CCR 1717.1(e)
224  B&PC 4059.5(f)(1)
225  B&PC 4104
226  B&PC 733

- Preventing the dispensing of a prescription when the pharmacist determines that the prescribed drug or device would cause a harmful drug interaction or would otherwise adversely affect the patient's medical condition.[227]

- Helping patients with limited or no English proficiency understand the information on the prescription container label in the patient's language, including the selected means to identify the patient's language and providing interpretive services in the patient's language.[228]

Hospital pharmacies and compounding pharmacies must have additional policies and procedures.[229, 230]

## DRUG STOCK

Drugs that are adulterated, misbranded, or expired cannot be purchased, traded, sold, or transferred. Adulteration involves the drug itself (the quality) and misbranding involves incorrect or missing information on the label. The drug stock must be clean, orderly, properly stored, properly labeled and in-date (i.e., not expired).

## Adulteration

Drugs are considered adulterated if:

- It is filthy, putrid, or decomposed.[231]

- It has been prepared, packed, or stored under unsanitary conditions where it may have become contaminated with filth, or where it can become dangerous to a person's health.

- It contains a drug recognized in official compendia, but its strength is different from official standards, or the purity or quality is lower than the official standards.

- It contains a drug not recognized in official compendia, but its strength is different from that listed on the label, or the quality or purity is lower than that listed on the label.

---

**Example**

A bottle is labeled to contain levothyroxine 100 mcg per tablet. The bottle is found to contain particulate contaminants in the tablets.

Purity is compromised (adulterated).

---

227   B&PC 733
228   CCR 1707.5
229   CCR 70263
230   CCR 1735.5
231   H&SC 111250

### Misbranding

Drugs are considered misbranded if:

- There is a lack of required information on the package and in the labeling (weight, count, warnings, use in specific groups, unsafe dosages, methods of use, treatment duration).

- There is any <u>false or misleading</u> product information, such as imitating the properties of another drug, or promising false cures.[232]

- There is a lack of special precautions needed to prevent decomposition that must be specified on the packaging, such as "keep in original container" or "protect from humidity and light".

- There is information that is illegible (cannot be read).

- The packaging does not contain the proprietary (branded) or established common name (as recognized by USP or Homeopathic Pharmacopoeia).

- The ingredients differ from the standard of strength, quality, or purity, as determined by the test laid out in the USP monograph.

- It does not contain the manufacturer and business location and packer or distributor.

- If there is improper packaging or improper or incomplete labeling of additives.

- If there is a deficiency in packaging according to the requirements of the Poison Prevention Packaging Act.

**Example**

An OTC capsule is labeled to contain caffeine and the "natural herbal" bitter orange, an adrenergic agonist similar to epinephrine. The container is labeled as an "easy and fast way to lose weight". Each capsule contains 10 mg of immediate-release amphetamine and 100 mg of caffeine and inactive ingredients.

The product is labeled to contain bitter orange, but actually contains amphetamine (misbranded).

## DELIVERY OF DRUGS TO A PHARMACY

### Delivery of Drugs to a Community/Outpatient Pharmacy

Drugs/devices are only delivered to the licensed premises, and signed for and received by a <u>pharmacist</u>.

A pharmacy can take delivery of drugs/devices when the pharmacy is closed and no pharmacist is on duty if all of the following requirements are met:

232   H&SC 111330

- The drugs are placed in a secure storage facility in the same building as the pharmacy.

- Only the PIC or a pharmacist designated by the PIC has access to the secure storage facility after drugs/devices have been delivered.

- The secure storage facility has a means of indicating whether it has been entered after the drugs/devices were delivered.

- The pharmacy maintains written P&Ps for the delivery of drugs/devices to a secure storage facility.

- The person delivering the drugs/devices leaves documents indicating the name and amount of each drug/device delivered.

The pharmacy is responsible for keeping records related to the delivery to the secure storage facility, and for the storage and security of the drugs/devices.

## Delivering Drugs to a Hospital Pharmacy

Drug/device deliveries are only delivered to the licensed premise and signed for and received by a pharmacist. Deliveries to a hospital pharmacy can be made to a <u>central receiving location</u> within the hospital. However, the drugs or devices must be delivered to the licensed pharmacy premise within <u>one working day</u> following the delivery, and the pharmacist on duty at that time must immediately <u>inventory</u> the drugs or devices.

A pharmacy can take delivery when the pharmacy is closed and no pharmacist is on duty if all of the following requirements are met:[233]

- The drugs/devices are placed in a secure storage facility in the same building as the pharmacy.

- Only the PIC or a pharmacist designated by the PIC has access to the secure storage facility after the drugs/devices have been delivered.

- The secure storage facility has a means of indicating whether it has been entered after the drugs/devices have been delivered.

- The pharmacy keeps written P&Ps for the delivery of drugs/devices to a secure storage facility.

- The agent delivering drugs/devices leaves documents indicating the name and amount of each drug/device delivered.

- The pharmacy is responsible for the drugs/devices, and for keeping records relating to the delivery of the drugs/devices.

233   B&PC 4059.5(f)

## DRUG STORAGE

All drug stock needs to be kept in a secure manner and in proper storage conditions with the right temperature, humidity, and light to keep it from becoming adulterated. Here is a list of other drugs that needs to be stored or handled in a different way. Most of these have to be kept separated from the drug stock to avoid misbranding and adulteration.

| DRUG | STORAGE |
|---|---|
| Controlled Drugs | Locked cabinet or dispersed throughout the other drug stock (on the shelves) |
| Investigational New Drugs | Separate from other drug stock |
| Repackaged or Resold Drugs | Separate from other drug stock, assigned BUD date |
| Recalled Drugs | Separate from other drug stock<br>■ Class I<br>■ Class II<br>■ Class III |
| Expired Drugs | Separate from other drug stock |
| Drug Samples | Separate from other drug stock, not allowed in retail pharmacies |

## PHARMACY SECURITY

All pharmacists on duty are responsible for the security of the pharmacy, including effective control against theft and diversion. The space must be secured by a physical and/or electronic barrier which can be locked and, preferably, be able to identify entry at all times. Access to non-pharmacy personnel should be kept to a minimum and any entry of non-pharmacy staff will be at the discretion of the pharmacist.

Pharmacies should install an alarm system, security cameras, "panic" buttons, and adequate exterior lighting and leave lights on after closing. There should be at least two employees on the premises during opening and closing. Security systems should include protection against outside and inside theft, including theft of electronic information and patient records. Staff members should be alert to suspicious activity and pay special attention to anyone who appears to be loitering, both inside and outside of your store. Only the pharmacists are allowed access to the pharmacy key, pharmacy interns cannot have access to the pharmacy key.

If a robbery does occur, do not resist, either verbally or physically. Remain calm and do exactly as you are told. Robbers are often armed and are focused on getting what they came to take. Take notice of the appearance of the robber so you can provide a description. When you can, write down what you observed. Sound the alarm as soon as possible and call the police. Lock doors immediately to prevent re-entry. Protect the crime scene until police arrive. Never try to apprehend or restrain the robber yourself.

## DRUG RECALLS

A drug recall occurs when a drug is removed from the market because it is defective or potentially harmful. The recall process for an FDA-approved drug is voluntary by the manufacturer, unless the FDA issues a mandatory recall to the manufacturer.

Pharmacies must be positioned to receive notification of recalls from multiple sources, which includes the FDA, federal, state or local law enforcement, and manufacturers or repackagers. If there are multiple locations in a central facility, the pharmacists involved with the recall will need to identify where the drug is located, and remove it from all patient care areas and storage locations, including in automated dispensing systems. If the recall involved specific batches or lot numbers, the pharmacist will need to have the stock checked and pull the recalled drug. The FDA does not mandate that the pharmacy contact the patient.

When the recalled drug is returned to the pharmacy, it is quarantined (separated) from other drugs prior to being returned or destroyed. Drugs that are quarantined for any reason (recalls, adulteration, expiration) must be labeled appropriately and placed in separate containers. Otherwise, they may be accidentally sent out to patients.

| CATEGORY | DESCRIPTION |
|---|---|
| Class I Recall | A situation in which there is a reasonable probability that the use or exposure will cause serious adverse health consequences or death. For example, a morphine tablet manufactured with ten times the amount of active ingredient would be subject to a Class I recall. The pharmacist must notify those patients' physicians, and keep a record of the physician notifications. The physician will be responsible for deciding whether his/her patients are to be contacted.[234] |
| Class II Recall | A situation in which use or exposure can cause temporary or reversible adverse health consequences or where the probability of harm is remote. For example, ketorolac injections have been recalled in 2010 and 2015 due to the possibility of particles in the vials. |
| Class III Recall | A situation in which use of or exposure is not likely to cause adverse health consequences. For example, the coloring on tablets may have been applied inconsistently. |

A pharmacy or outsourcing facility that issues a recall notice about its compounded drug preparation must contact the recipient pharmacy, prescriber, or patient of the recalled drug and the board within 12 hours and 24 hours (respectively) of the recall notice if both of the following apply:[235, 236, 237]

- Use of or exposure to the recalled compounded preparation can cause serious adverse effects or death.

- The recalled compounded preparation was dispensed, or is intended for use, in California.

234 http://www.fda.gov/ICECI/ComplianceManuals/CompliancePolicyGuidanceManual/ucm074365.htm (accessed 2018 Feb 22).
235 B&PC 4126.9
236 B&PC 4127.8
237 B&PC 4129.9

A recall notice for a compounded drug preparation must be made as follows:

- If the recalled drug was dispensed directly to the patient, the notice must be made to the patient.

- If the recalled drug was dispensed directly to the prescriber, the notice must be made to the prescriber, who must ensure the patient is notified.

- If the recalled drug was dispensed directly to a pharmacy, the notice must be made to the pharmacy, who must notify the prescriber or patient, as appropriate. If the pharmacy notifies the prescriber, the prescriber must ensure the patient is notified.

If the pharmacy is made aware that a patient has been harmed by using a compounded product prepared by the pharmacy, the pharmacy must report the event to the federal FDA *MedWatch* within 72 hours. If the outsourcing facility is made aware that a patient has been harmed by using a compounded product prepared by the facility, the facility must report the event to the federal FDA *MedWatch* within 15 calendar days.[238]

## DRUG AND VACCINE SHORTAGES

Information regarding drug and vaccine shortage are available at the following websites:

American Society of Health-System Pharmacists: *www.ashp.org/drugshortages*

Food and Drug Administration: *www.fda.gov/drugs/drugsafety/drugshortages/*

Centers for Disease Control and Prevention: *www.cdc.gov/vaccines/vac-gen/shortages/*

238   *21 CFR 310.305(c)(1)(i)*

## RETURN, DISPOSAL, OR REUSE OF DRUGS

### Pharmacies Returning Drugs to the Supplier

The FDA permits pharmacies to return drugs to wholesalers and manufacturers as long as there is proper recordkeeping.[239]

For <u>schedule III – V drugs</u>, the pharmacist must maintain a <u>written record</u> showing:

1. The date of the transaction.

2. The name, strength, dosage form, and quantity of the controlled substance.

3. The supplier or manufacturer's name, address, and registration number.

A <u>DEA Form 222</u> or its electronic equivalent must accompany the transfer of <u>schedule II drugs</u>. If the Form 222 is used, the wholesaler will keep Copy 3, and send Copies 1 and 2 to the pharmacy, which is acting as the "supplier". The pharmacy will forward Copy 2 to the DEA.

### Registrants Sending Controlled Substances to Reverse Distributor

A pharmacy can transfer controlled substances to a DEA registered reverse distributor who handles the disposal of controlled substances. In no case should drugs be sent to the DEA unless the registrant has received prior approval from the DEA.

When a pharmacy transfers <u>schedule II drugs</u> to a reverse distributor for destruction, the reverse distributor must issue an official order form (<u>DEA Form 222</u>) or the electronic equivalent to the pharmacy. The reverse distributor will keep Copy 3, and send Copies 1 and 2 to the pharmacy, which is acting as the "supplier". The pharmacy will forward Copy 2 to the DEA. When <u>schedules III – V drugs</u> are transferred to a reverse distributor for destruction, the pharmacy must maintain a <u>record of distribution</u> that lists the drug name, dosage form, strength, quantity, and date transferred.

The DEA registered <u>reverse distributor</u> who will destroy the controlled substances is responsible for completing a <u>DEA Form 41</u>.[240]

---

239   B&PC 4081
240   http://www.deadiversion.usdoj.gov/21cfr_reports/surrend/41_form.pdf (accessed 2018 Feb 16).

OMB APPROVAL NO. 1117-0007                                          Expiration Date 9/30/2017

**U. S. DEPARTMENT OF JUSTICE – DRUG ENFORCEMENT ADMINISTRATION**
# REGISTRANT RECORD OF CONTROLLED SUBSTANCES DESTROYED
**FORM DEA-41**

## A. REGISTRANT INFORMATION

Registered Name:                                          DEA Registration Number:

Registered Address:

City:                                  State:          Zip Code:

Telephone Number:                                        Contact Name:

## B. ITEM DESTROYED
### 1. Inventory

| | National Drug Code or DEA Controlled Substances Code Number | Batch Number | Name of Substance | Strength | Form | Pkg. Qty. | Number of Full Pkgs. | Partial Pkg. Count | Total Destroyed |
|---|---|---|---|---|---|---|---|---|---|
| *Examples* | 16590-598-60 | N/A | Kadian | 60mg | Capsules | 60 | 2 | 0 | 120 Capsules |
| | 0555-0767-02 | N/A | Adderall | 5mg | Tablet | 100 | 0 | 83 | 83 Tablets |
| | 9050 | B02120312 | Codeine | N/A | Bulk | 1.25 kg | N/A | N/A | 1.25 kg |
| 1. | | | | | | | | | |
| 2. | | | | | | | | | |
| 3. | | | | | | | | | |
| 4. | | | | | | | | | |
| 5. | | | | | | | | | |
| 6. | | | | | | | | | |
| 7. | | | | | | | | | |

### 2. Collected Substances

| | Returned Mail-Back Package | Sealed Inner Liner | Unique Identification Number | Size of Sealed Inner Liner | Quantity of Packages(s)/Liner(s) Destroyed |
|---|---|---|---|---|---|
| *Examples* | X | | MBP1106, MBP1108 - MBP1110, MBP112 | N/A | 5 |
| | | X | CRL1007 - CRL1027 | 15 gallon | 21 |
| | | X | CRL1201 | 5 gallon | 1 |
| 1. | | | | | |
| 2. | | | | | |
| 3. | | | | | |
| 4. | | | | | |
| 5. | | | | | |
| 6. | | | | | |
| 7. | | | | | |

**Form DEA-41**                    *See instructions on reverse (page 2) of form.*

*Image courtesy of the Drug Enforcement Administration*

## Pharmacies Donating Drugs for Redistribution

California permit prescription drugs in single use or sealed packaging from <u>skilled nursing facility, home healthcare, board and care, or mail order</u> to be donated to a drug repository and distribution program.[241] This helps offset the costs of providing healthcare to eligible patients with a valid prescription. The laws include some restrictions to ensure drug integrity:[242]

- <u>No controlled substances can be donated.</u>

- Must be <u>unused</u> and <u>unexpired</u>

- Are in unopened, tamper-evident packaging or modified unit dose containers with lot numbers and expiration dates.

- Have not been adulterated or misbranded.

- Drugs that require refrigeration must be stored, packaged and transported at appropriate temperatures.

- Were received directly from a manufacturer or wholesaler.

- Were returned from a health facility to which the drugs were originally issued.

- Were never in the possession of a patient or member of the public.

Pharmacies can also operate a drug repository and distribution program. Pharmacies that exists solely to operate the repository and distribution program can repackage donated drugs.[243]


## Patients Returning Drugs to the Pharmacy

Pharmacies can accept returned prescription drugs from patients in certain situations (e.g., the wrong drug was dispensed), but the returned drug cannot be returned to stock or dispensed to another patient. The pharmacy must dispose of the returned drug properly.


## Patients Disposing Drugs

It is important to dispose of drugs properly to <u>avoid drug abuse, accidental ingestion, and environmental pollution</u>. The board has adopted the federal Drug Enforcement Administration (DEA) regulations on drug take-back services.[244] There are a variety of safe and responsible ways to dispose of drugs through <u>law enforcement-sponsored take back events, collection bin/receptacles</u>, and <u>mail back packages</u>. In certain situations, it is also acceptable for patients to throw away drugs in the household trash, sink, or toilet.

241   H&SC 150202.5
242   H&SC 150204
243   H&SC 150204(i)(2)
244   CCR 1776

Pharmacies can voluntarily register with the DEA to take back unwanted drugs from patients by installing a collection bin. The patient should place the drugs directly into the collection bin themselves, preventing the pharmacy staff from knowing what is being returned. Once drugs are deposited into a collection bin by a patient, they cannot to be removed, counted, sorted or otherwise individually handled. Controlled substances can be commingled (mixed together) in a collection bin with non-controlled drugs. Sharps and needles (e.g., insulin syringes) and illicit drugs cannot be placed in the bin. These collection bins are only to be used by patients and their caregivers. Pharmacies cannot use the collection bins to dispose of their own expired or recalled drugs.

The following notifications must be made to the board:

| NOTIFICATION TO THE BOARD | TIMEFRAME |
|---|---|
| Establishment of drug take back service | Within 30 days |
| Discontinuation of drug take back service | Within 30 days |
| Any tampering with a collection bin | Within 14 days |
| Theft of deposited drugs | Within 14 days |
| Any tampering, damage or theft of a removed liner | Within 14 days |
| Disclosure of service and location of each receptacle | Annually, at time of facility license renewal |

Pharmacies can also provide pre-paid, pre-addressed mailing envelopes for patients to return drugs to an authorized destruction location.[245] The patient puts the medications into the envelope and drops off the package at the post office. The package has a plain wrapper, without any markings or other information that indicates what is inside the envelope. The package is waterproof, spill-proof, tamper-evident, tear-resistant, and sealable. The package has a unique identification number that enables the package to be tracked.

In the absence of these programs, the patient could also properly dispose of their unwanted drugs in the household trash if certain precautions are taken. The patients should dispose of drugs in the household trash following these steps.[246]

■ Remove the drugs from their original containers and mix them with an undesirable substance, such as dirt, used coffee grounds, or kitty litter (this makes the drug less appealing to children and pets, and unrecognizable to people who can intentionally go through the trash seeking drugs).

■ Place the mixture in a sealable bag, empty can, or other container.

■ Discard in the trash.

In most cases, drugs should not be disposed of by flushing it down the sink or toilet because it can contaminate the water supply or soil. However, some medications can be particularly

245   CCR 1776.2
246   http://www.calrecycle.ca.gov/HomeHazWaste/Medications/Household.htm (accessed 2018 Feb 16).

fatal if accidentally ingested by others (especially children and pets), causing respiratory depression, and possibly leading to death. For these reasons, FDA recommends patients to <u>flush</u> certain drugs (e.g., oxycodone, fentanyl patch, meperidine, methadone, morphine, and *Percocet*) <u>down the sink or toilet</u> so they can immediately and permanently remove this risk from their home if it is not possible to return these medicines through a take-back program, collection receptacle, or mail-back program. The FDA feels that the health risks from accidental ingestion outweighs any health or environmental risks due to flushing. See the FDA website for the complete list of drugs.[247]

## RECORDKEEPING AND REPORTING REQUIREMENTS

| RECORD | MAINTAINED FOR AT LEAST: |
|---|---|
| Hospital pharmacy chart order records for controlled substances | 7 years |
| Patient acknowledgment of HIPAA | 6 years |
| Transaction information, history, and statement for most prescription drugs as required under the Drug Supply Chain Security Act | 6 years |
| Certificate of completion for continuing education | 4 years |
| Biennial controlled substances inventory | 3 years |
| Community or clinic pharmacy prescriptions | 3 years |
| Hospital pharmacy chart order records for non-controlled drugs | 3 years |
| Controlled substance inventory | 3 years |
| DEA forms 222, power of attorney forms | 3 years |
| Purchase invoices for all prescription drugs | 3 years |
| Self-assessment forms | 3 years |
| Record documenting return of drugs to wholesaler or manufacturer | 3 years |
| Record documenting transfers or sales to other pharmacies, licensees and prescribers | 3 years |
| Theft and loss reports of controlled substances (DEA Form 106) | 3 years |
| Pseudoephedrine, ephedrine, phenylpropanolamine, and norpseudoephedrine sale logs | 2 years |
| Patient medication profile | 1 year |
| Medication error/quality assurance reports | 1 year |

| ACTION/EVENT | REPORTING TIME PERIOD |
|---|---|
| Change of pharmacist address or name | Within 30 days |
| Change of pharmacist-in-charge | Within 30 days |
| Changes in the pharmacy permit | Within 30 days |
| Theft by or impairment of a licensee | Within 14 days |
| Loss/theft of controlled drugs | Report to DEA immediately (one business day) Report to California Board of Pharmacy within 30 days |
| Bankruptcy, insolvency, receivership | Immediately |

247   http://www.fda.gov/Drugs/ResourcesForYou/Consumers/BuyingUsingMedicineSafely/EnsuringSafeUseofMedicine/SafeDisposalofMedicines/ucm186187.htm#Flush_List (accessed 2018 Feb 16).

| TASK | FREQUENCY |
|------|-----------|
| Controlled substances inventory | Every 2 years |
| Self-assessment form | Every odd-numbered year before July 1st. |
| | Within 30 days, when there is a new pharmacy permit, a change in PIC, or a change in pharmacy location. |
| Pharmacist continuing education (30 hours) | Every 2 years, except first cycle |
| Submitting dispensing data to CURES | Weekly |
| Medication error investigation | Within 2 days of error |

All <u>drug acquisition</u> (e.g., invoices) and <u>disposition records</u> (e.g., prescription records, chart orders) are kept for at least <u>three years</u>. All schedule II drug records and inventories are kept separate from all others.

## Paper Prescription Recordkeeping System for Controlled Substances

Pharmacies have two options for filing paper prescription records:

### Paper Prescriptions Records Option 1 (Three separate files):

■ A file for schedule II drugs dispensed.

■ A file for schedules III, IV and V drugs dispensed.

■ A file for all non-controlled drugs dispensed.

### Paper Prescriptions Records Option 2 (Two separate files):

■ A file for all schedule II drugs dispensed.

■ A file for all other drugs dispensed (non-controlled and schedules III, IV and V drugs).

If this method is used, a prescription for a schedule III, IV or V drug must be made readily retrievable by use of a <u>red "C" stamp at least one inch high</u>. This enables a person to quickly flip through the records and pull them out from the rest. The red "C" is waived if the pharmacy has an electronic prescription recordkeeping system, which can identify controlled drugs by prescription number.

## Electronic Prescription Recordkeeping System for Controlled Substances

Pharmacies have one option for electronic prescription records. Electronic records are also kept for <u>three years</u>. The system needs the capacity to sort by prescriber name, patient name, drug dispensed, and date filled.

## Hospital Chart Orders

A medication or chart order is written by a prescriber for immediate administration to a patient in a hospital or other institutional setting. The prescriber enters the medication order, the order is sent to the pharmacy for dispensing, and the nurse directly administers the drug to the patient. The drug is never in the possession of the patient. Records of chart orders for non-controlled substances must be kept for 3 years and chart orders for controlled substances must be kept for 7 years.[248]

## DEA Controlled Substances Inventory

Before opening a new pharmacy, there must be a complete inventory of all controlled substances. If there is no stock of controlled substances on hand, the registrant needs a record that shows a zero inventory. For regular inventories, the pharmacy needs to record the controlled substances currently on hand. The inventory is taken minimally on a biennial basis (every two years). Pharmacies must maintain inventory records at each location. The inventory records of schedule II drugs must be kept separate from all other controlled substances. There is no requirement to submit a copy of the inventory to the DEA. If the pharmacist suspects a loss, the inventory is taken as soon as possible to confirm the loss.

Inventory is counted at either the beginning or close of business. Inventory is not performed during business hours because inventory is changing due to medications being dispensed to patients. The records must be maintained in written, typewritten, or printed format. Inventory taken with a recording device must be reduced to writing promptly. The final form of the record must be on paper and must contain:

■ Date of the inventory

■ If the inventory was taken at the beginning or close of business

■ Names of controlled substances

■ Dosage forms and strengths

■ Number of dosage units or volume in each container (see below on how to count)

■ Number of commercial containers

If a drug becomes scheduled or changes schedules, pharmacies must inventory newly scheduled drugs on the date the scheduling became effective:

■ For sealed, unopened containers of all controlled substances, an exact count is needed. There is no need to open a sealed container, using the unit count listed on the manufacturer's drug container is sufficient.

- For <u>opened</u> containers of controlled substances:

  ❏ All schedule <u>I and II</u> containers require an <u>exact count</u>

  ❏ Schedule <u>III – V</u> containers that hold 1000 dosage units or <u>less</u> can be <u>estimated</u>

  ❏ Schedule <u>III – V</u> containers that hold <u>more</u> than 1000 dosage units require an <u>exact count</u>

The inventory must be available for inspection for three years.[249]

## Off-Site Storage of Records

The board can grant waivers to allow off-site storage of records.[250] All records stored off-site must be kept in a <u>secure area</u> to prevent unauthorized access. Examples of reasonable storage areas are at records maintenance facilities or commercial storage centers. The board requests that the waiver, if approved, be kept in the pharmacy. If the waiver for off-site storage of records is approved, a <u>signed copy</u> of the form will be returned to the pharmacy within <u>30 days.</u> Off-site storage of records is not allowed until the board approves the waiver. A new waiver for off-site storage of records is needed if the records are moved to a different off-site location. The pharmacy must be able to produce the records within <u>2 business days upon the request</u> of the board or another authorized officer of the law.[251, 252]

Prescription records are kept for 3 years total. Prescriptions for <u>non-controlled substances</u> must be kept <u>at the pharmacy</u> for at least <u>1 year.</u> After that, the pharmacy can choose to store the prescriptions off-site for another 2 years. This is often done because there is not enough room in the pharmacy to keep all the paperwork. After 3 years has passed since the prescription was last dispensed, the pharmacy can throw the prescriptions away altogether, although many pharmacies choose to keep the prescriptions for longer. Prescriptions for <u>controlled substances</u> must be kept <u>at the pharmacy</u> for at least <u>2 years</u>. After that, the pharmacy can choose to store the prescriptions off-site for another year.

## Drug Pedigrees

There is an increasing prevalence of counterfeit, misbranded, adulterated, and diverted prescription drugs showing up in the United States. To prevent these drugs from entering the legitimate drug supply, the federal Drug Supply Chain Security Act was passed in 2013, which outlines steps to build a system to <u>track and trace</u> drugs as they are distributed within the United States.[253] This requirement applies to <u>prescription</u> drugs intended for <u>human</u> use. Many products are exempt, including: over-the-counter drugs, medical devices, active pharmaceutical ingredients, veterinary drugs, blood products for transfusion, radioactive drugs, imaging drugs, certain intravenous products, certain medical gases (e.g., oxygen), homeopathic drugs and compounded preparations.

249   CCR 1718
250   CCR 1707
251   B&PC 4105
252   http://www.pharmacy.ca.gov/forms/offsite_storage.pdf (accessed 2018 Feb 16).
253   https://www.fda.gov/downloads/Drugs/GuidanceComplianceRegulatoryInformation/Guidances/UCM453225.pdf (accessed 2018 Feb 16).

Manufacturers, wholesale distributors, pharmacies and repackagers (collectively referred to as "trading partners") are required to provide the subsequent purchaser with product tracing information when engaging in transactions involving certain prescription drugs. This means that anytime the drug is moved from one place to another, paperwork must follow.

Pharmacies must be able to capture and maintain transaction information (TI), transaction history (TH), and a transaction statement (TS), in paper or electronic form, for each drug product received for six years from the date of the transaction.[254] There are some situations that are exempt from this requirement, including dispensing drugs to a patient, providing drugs to a practitioner for office use, and distributing samples.

| TERM | DEFINITION |
|---|---|
| Transaction history | The transaction history is a statement in paper or electronic form, including the transaction information for each prior transaction going back to the manufacturer of the product. |
| Transaction information | The transaction information includes the:<br><br>■ Proprietary or established name or names of the product<br>■ Strength and dosage form of the product<br>■ National Drug Code number of the product<br>■ Container size<br>■ Number of containers<br>■ Lot number of the product<br>■ Date of the transaction<br>■ Date of the shipment, if more than 24 hours after the date of the transaction<br>■ Business name and address of the person from whom ownership is being transferred<br>■ Business name and address of the person to whom ownership is being transferred |
| Transaction statement | The transaction statement is a statement, in paper or electronic form, that the entity transferring ownership in a transaction:<br><br>■ Is authorized<br>■ Received the product from a person that is authorized<br>■ Received transaction information and a transaction statement from the prior owner of the product<br>■ Did not knowingly ship a suspect or illegitimate product<br>■ Had systems and processes in place to comply with verification requirements<br>■ Did not knowingly provide false transaction information<br>■ Did not knowingly alter the transaction history |

254   http://www.pharmacy.ca.gov/publications/15_fall_script.pdf (accessed 2018 Feb 16).

## INSPECTION OF A PHARMACY

Board inspectors assess if pharmacies are compliant with federal and state laws and regulations. The pharmacy can face disciplinary actions if legal requirements are not met. The pharmacist-in-charge must complete the self-assessment form <u>before July 1 of every odd-numbered year</u> to assess the pharmacy's compliance with the law. An action plan must be noted to correct any non-compliance. The form is not sent anywhere, but kept on file in the pharmacy in case an inspector wants to see it. There is a self-assessment form for different practice settings: community/hospital outpatient, compounding, and hospital inpatient. These self-assessment forms are important to review for practice and for the exam.

Whenever the controlled substance prescription is removed from pharmacy records by a peace officer, agent of the Attorney General, or inspector of the board, or investigator of the Division of Investigation of the Department of Consumer Affairs for the purpose of investigation or as evidence, the officer or inspector or investigator must give to the pharmacist a <u>receipt</u>.[255] The pharmacy should make a copy of the prescription, give the original to the officer/agent/inspector, and keep the duplicate copy.

## MANDATORY REPORTING OF ABUSE AND NEGLECT

Each person licensed by the board (pharmacists, intern pharmacists and technicians) are "mandated reporters" of child abuse, elder abuse and neglect. Pharmacy staff have regular contact with vulnerable people, including children and elders. A report should be made when there is a reason to believe that a child/elder is a victim of abuse or neglect. The mandated reporters must phone law enforcement or protective services as soon as they can, and prepare and send a written report within <u>2 working days</u> or <u>36 hours</u> of receiving the information concerning the incident. Failure to do so is a misdemeanor, punishable by up to six months in a county jail and/or a fine of $1,000.

255  *H&SC 11195*

# 5

# Appendix

## AUXILIARY LABELS, ORAL FORMULATIONS

This list should not be considered exhaustive, but it does represent major categories for auxiliary labels.

| LABEL | COMMENT |
|---|---|
| Caution: Federal Law PROHIBITS the transfer of this drug to any person other than the patient for whom it was prescribed. | The label of schedule II, III, or IV drugs must have the following warning: "Caution: Federal law prohibits the transfer of this drug to any person other than the patient for whom it was prescribed." |
| SHAKE WELL BEFORE USING | Shake Well (all suspensions, most asthma aerosol inhalers and nasal steroid sprays, lidocaine viscous topical liquid). |
| REFRIGERATE | Refrigerate or Keep in Refrigerator; Do not Freeze (antibiotic suspensions): amoxicillin (refrigeration not required, but improves taste), cefpodoxime (*Vantin*), cefprozil (*Cefzil*), cefuroxime (*Ceftin*), ceftibuten (*Cedax*), cephalexin (Keflex), erythromycin/benzoyl peroxide gel (*Benzamycin*), erythromycin/sulfisoxazole, penicillin V. |
| | Others: adalimumab (*Humira*), dronabinol (*Marinol, Syndros*), etanercept (*Enbrel*), calcitonin NS (*Miacalcin*), chlorambucil (*Leukeran*), ESAs (*Epogen, Aranesp, Procrit*), etoposide (*VePesid*), filgrastim (*Neupogen*), insulins (that patient is not using), interferons (all), nystatin pastilles (*Mycostatin*), somatropin (*Genotropin, Humatrope*), lopinavir/ritonavir solution (*Kaletra*), alprostadil (*MUSE,* reconstituted *Caverject*), ritonavir softgels (*Norvir*), sandostatin (*Octreotide*), sirolimus solution (*Rapamune*), teriparatide (*Forteo*), thyrolar (*Liotrix*), lactobacillus (*Visbiome*), *NuvaRing*, promethazine suppositories, typhoid oral capsules (*Vivotif Berna*), formoterol (*Foradil* – prior to dispensing, patient can keep at room temp), dornase alfa (*Pulmozyme* — room temp only if < 24 hours). |
| | Eyedrops: latanoprost (unopened *Xalatan* bottles), tafluprost (*Zioptan* – opened pouch good for 30 days room temp), trifluridine (*Viroptic*). |
| FOR EXTERNAL USE ONLY | For External Use Only (topicals), may require: "For the Eye", "For the Ear", "For the Nose," "For Rectal Use Only," "For Vaginal Use Only," "Not to be taken by Mouth" |
| IMPORTANT FINISH ALL THIS MEDICATION UNLESS OTHERWISE DIRECTED BY PRESCRIBER | Finish all this medication, unless otherwise directed by prescriber (antibiotics, antivirals, antifungals). |

| LABEL | COMMENT |
|---|---|
| May cause DROWSINESS ALCOHOL may INTENSIFY this effect. Use care when operating a car or dangerous machinery | May cause drowsiness. May impair the ability to drive or operate machinery.<br><br>Includes analgesics with CNS effects, antipsychotics, some antidepressants including mirtazapine (*Remeron*) and trazodone (*Desyrel*), dopamine agonists (ropinirole, etc.), antihistamines, antinauseants, anticonvulsants, muscle relaxants, antihypertensives with CNS effects, all C II, III, IV or V depressant or narcotic drugs, including hypnotics-controlled & not controlled. |
| MAY CAUSE BLURRED VISION | May affect vision. Includes amiodarone, anticholinergics, ethambutol, hydroxychloroquine, isoniazid, isotretinoin, PDE 5 inhibitors (sildenafil, others), scopolamine patch, tamoxifen, telithromycin, voriconazole (*VFEND*).<br><br>Note: many drugs cause blurry or doubled vision (diplopia) if toxic, including alcohol and CNS depressants. Digoxin can cause yellow halos if toxic. |
| DO NOT DRINK ALCOHOLIC BEVERAGES when taking this medication. | Do not use alcohol while taking this medicine. Includes disulfiram, tinidazole, metronidazole (both of these avoid alcohol to 48 hrs after last dose), nitrates, opioids (all, but special warning for *Avinza, Opana*), tramadol, tapentadol (*Nucynta*), benzodiazepines, barbiturates, non-benzodiazepine hypnotics (zolpidem, etc.), anticonvulsants, antipsychotics, some antidepressants, skeletal muscle relaxants, insulin, metformin, sulfonylureas. |
| YOU SHOULD AVOID PROLONGED OR EXCESSIVE EXPOSURE TO DIRECT AND/OR ARTIFICIAL SUNLIGHT WHILE TAKING THIS MEDICINE | Avoid prolonged exposure to direct and/or artificial sunlight while using this medicine. Includes sulfa antibiotics, fluoroquinolones, tetracyclines, topical retinoids (newer ones less risk), isotretinoin (oral), ritonavir & a few other HIV drugs, NSAIDs (piroxicam, diclofenac, some risk with ibuprofen and naproxen), metronidazole, isoniazid, diuretics. |
| Take Medication On An EMPTY STOMACH 1 Hour Before or 2 to 3 Hours After a Meal Unless Otherwise Directed By Your Dr. | Take on an empty stomach. Includes ampicillin, efavirenz (*Sustiva/Atripla* – empty stomach, preferably at bedtime), bisphosphonates (at least half hour before breakfast or 60 minutes for *Boniva*), captopril (1 hour before meals), didanosine (*Videx*), indinavir (*Crixivan*), iron (if tolerated), PPIs (variable times, but all before eating), tadalafil and sildenafil (light meal, avoid fatty food), levothyroxine (30-60 mins before breakfast or 3-4 hours after last meal), *Opana*, mycophenolate (*CellCept*), tacrolimus extended release (*Astagraf XL, Envarsus XR*), voriconazole (*VFEND*), zafirlukast. |
| TAKE WITH FOOD | Take with food. Includes atazanavir (*Reyataz*), carvedilol (*Coreg*), itraconazole capsules, metformin (IR with breakfast and dinner, XR with dinner) lovastatin (with dinner), fenofibrate and derivatives (*Lofibra, Lipofen, Fenoglide*), niacin, gemfibrozil (*Lopid* – 30 min before breakfast and dinner), phosphate binders (when eating), NSAIDs, opioids (except *Opana*), steroids, metoprolol tartrate (*Lopressor*) |
| MEDICATION SHOULD BE TAKEN WITH PLENTY OF WATER | Take with full glass of water. Includes sulfamethoxazole/trimethoprim (*Bactrim*), bisphosphonates, sulfasalazine (*Azulfidine* – take with water & food).<br><br>Note: Drugs can get "stuck" going down, especially if dysphagia is present. It is preferable to take most with a full glass of water. |
| Avoid taking this medication with grapefruit or grapefruit juice. | Do not eat grapefruit or drink grapefruit juice at any time while using this medicine. Includes lovastatin, simvastatin, atorvastatin, amiodarone, buspirone, carbamazepine, cyclosporine, tacrolimus, diazepam, triazolam, verapamil, nicardipine, felodipine, nisoldipine, nifedipine, telithromycin |
| WARNING: DO NOT USE IF YOU ARE PREGNANT, PLAN TO BECOME PREGNANT OR WHILE BREASTFEEDING. CONSULT YOUR DOCTOR OR PHARMACIST. | Danger in pregnancy. If you are pregnant or considering becoming pregnant talk to your doctor before using this medicine. Includes ACE inhibitors, angiotensin receptor blockers, renin inhibitors, carbamazepine, isotretinoin, lithium, NSAIDs, phenytoin, phenobarbital, topiramate, valproic acid, ribavirin, misoprostol, methotrexate, leflunomide, statins, dutasteride, finasteride, warfarin, lenalidomide, thalidomide. |

| LABEL | COMMENT |
|---|---|
| **MAY CAUSE DISCOLORATION** OF THE URINE OR FECES | May cause discoloration of the urine, skin and sweat. May stain contact lenses and clothing. Includes entacapone, levodopa, metronidazole, nitrofurantoin, phenazopyridine, rifampin, sulfasalazine, doxorubicin, mitoxantrone, propofol. |
| CHECK FOR PEANUT OR SOY ALLERGY | Check for peanut or soy allergy. Includes progesterone (*Prometrium* only, not in other formulations), clevidipine (*Cleviprex*), and propofol. |
| DO NOT TAKE DAIRY PRODUCTS ANTACIDS OR IRON PREPARATIONS WITHIN ONE HOUR OF THIS MEDICATION | Separate from dairy products, calcium, magnesium or iron tablets, antacids. Includes tetracyclines, quinolones. |
| **SWALLOW WHOLE** DO NOT CRUSH | Do not chew or crush. Swallow whole. Enteric coated formulations (bisacodyl, others), any drug that ends with XR, ER, LA, SR, CR, CRT, SA, TR, TD, or has 24 in the name, or the ending "–cont" (for controlled release, such as *MS Contin* or *Oxycontin*), and timecaps and sprinkles.<br><br>Note: Can cut metoprolol extended-release and levodopa-carbidopa SR at the score line (for half the dose), but cannot crush or chew. |
| Warning: If your stool becomes soft and watery after using this antibiotic, contact your doctor immediately. | Persistent diarrhea due to colitis may occur weeks after using the medication—report to your doctor immediately if this occurs. Includes clindamycin, broad-spectrum antibiotics. |
| When taking this medication the effectiveness of birth control pills are decreased. Use additional and/or alternate methods of birth control. - 1989 API | Warning: This Medicine May Make Birth Control Less Effective. Includes barbiturates (phenobarbital, etc.), St. Johns wort, some HIV drugs (some of the protease inhibitors, NNRTIs), ampicillin, tetracycline, rifampin, rifapentine, griseofulvin, anticonvulsants (topiramate, lamotrigine, carbamazepine, primidone, phenytoin, oxcarbazepine), bosentan |

## AUXILIARY LABELS, INTRAVENOUS FORMULATIONS

This list should not be considered exhaustive, but it does represent major categories for auxiliary labels. See the IV Drug Storage, Compatibility, Administration & Degradation chapter.

For further discussion of high-alert medications refer to the Medication Safety & Quality Improvement chapter in the RxPrep Course Book. These are standard labels; labels should be chosen & customized to meet the specific institution's needs.

The Institute for Safe Medication Practices (ISMP) defines **HIGH ALERT** medications as those that have **HIGH RISK of causing significant patient harm when they are used in error**. Safeguards must be put in place to reduce the risk of errors, including the proper use of labeling.

**High alert medications include:**

- **Adrenergic agonists** (such as epinephrine)—specify drug dose in mg and use caution to note that epinephrine 1:1000 is 1 mg/mL and 1:10,000 is 0.1 mg/mL; there have been fatal mix-ups.

- **Adrenergic antagonists** ("beta blockers" such as propranolol)—some of the errors involved giving the same dose IV as the oral medication, when the IV dose is much lower, such as ~5 mg IV metoprolol for 50 mg of the oral dose. Use caution (monitor) with low HR or hypotension and with additive drugs that lower HR and BP.

- **Anesthetic agents** (such as midazolam (*Versed*), dexmedetomidine (*Precedex*) and propofol (*Diprivan*)—these are common ICU agents used to sedate patients on ventilators. They lower HR and cause hypotension—over-sedation can be fatal. Only skilled staff can administer and monitor, via a protocol that defines the rate (dosed by weight and desired sedation level) and enforces continuous monitoring of BP, airway & sedation level.

- **Antiarrhythmics** (such as amiodarone)—should be administered by protocol that defines LD, infusion rate & requirement for cardiac (ECG) and BP monitoring.

- **Unfractionated heparin**—administered via protocol that includes required baseline labs (INR, aPTT, CBC), requires discontinuation of all drugs that can increase bleeding risk, states frequency for monitoring, uses weight-based dosing for initial bolus and infusion rate, sets goal aPTT by condition, states rate adjustments based on aPTT, monitoring for symptoms of bleeding, and protamine dosing (if needed), and protocol required for use of other antithrombotics, including argatroban (commonly used as alternative agent for HIT), bivalirudin, alteplase, reteplase & eptifibatide, and anticoagulants such as warfarin, dabigatran and rivaroxaban (see Medication Safety & Quality Improvement and Anticoagulation chapters in RxPrep Course Book).

- **Insulin**—including in IVPBs, protocol should include initial infusion rate, rate adjustment based on BG, BG monitoring frequency, K+ monitoring and when to notify physician (usually BG >500 mg/dL, and if hypoglycemic). ISMP is now recommending hospitals stop stocking insulin pens due to contamination issues arising from using the same pen device in multiple patients.

- **Inotropic medications** (IV, including digoxin, milrinone)—prior to administration and frequently during administration monitor BP, HR and hemodynamic parameters. Monitor fluids, administration rate & urine output.

- **Opioids**—need to screen and monitor patients at risk for oversedation and respiratory depression. Conversion support system should help convert between agents. Use tall man lettering and separate look-alike/sound-alike agents.

| | |
|---|---|
| 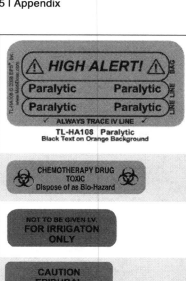<br>**TL-HA108 Paralytic**<br>**Black Text on Orange Background** | Neuromuscular blocking agents (including cisatracurium, vecuronium, succinylcholine, rocuronium, pancuronium)—can only be given to a patient who is ALREADY on BOTH an analgesic (such as fentanyl) and an anesthetic (such as propofol—see above) with pain and sedation assessed continuously. Also elevate head of bed and regularly assess possibility of weaning off ventilator. |
| CHEMOTHERAPY DRUG TOXIC Dispose of as Bio-Hazard | Chemotherapeutic agents require special packaging and labeling for proper handling of the medication and proper disposal of the bag and tubing. (Alternative wording is: Chemotherapy: Dispose of Properly.) |
| NOT TO BE GIVEN I.V. FOR IRRIGATON ONLY | Any type of irrigation should be labeled so that it is NOT administered intravenously (Includes peritoneal dialysis irrigation solution, saline & sterile water irrigation solution). |
| CAUTION EPIDURAL NARCOTIC | Epidural or intrathecal solution should be labeled to decrease risk of administration via an incorrect route. |
| HYPERTONIC SALINE CAUTION. HIGH ALERT | Sodium chloride for injection, hypertonic (greater than 0.9% concentration)—refer to Medication Safety & Quality Improvement chapter in RxPrep Course Book for safety requirements for hypertonic saline. NO preparation on units, keep off general medicine floors. Administer per protocol only. |
| DO NOT REFRIGERATE | Metronidazole (*Flagyl*), sulfamethoxazole/ trimethoprim (*Bactrim*), phenylephrine (*Neosynephrine*), hydralazine, moxifloxacin (*Avelox*), acetaminophen (*Ofirmev*) & esomeprazole (*Nexium*) |
| PROTECT FROM LIGHT | Amiodarone, amphotericin, ciprofloxacin, furosemide, levofloxacin, metronidazole, nitroprusside, phytonadione, epoprostenol, doxycycline, micafungin. |
| POTASSIUM ADDED | IV fluids with potassium added. If KCl is given to correct hypokalemia, a protocol should contain the maximum rate of infusion & cardiac and K+ monitoring requirements. Concentrated potassium (or other electrolytes) should NOT be in the patient care units. All additive sources of potassium should be considered in any patient receiving potassium. See Medication Safety chapter in RxPrep Course Book for further discussion. |
| ADMINISTER BY INTRAMUSCULAR (IM) INJECTION | IM only for promethazine injectable. Promethazine injection is difficult with any route, but worse with IV administration and should be given by IM only (SC and IV contraindicated) due to tissue irritation and damage. Contraindicated in patients < 2 years old due to risk of fatal respiratory depression. |
| FOR CENTRAL LINE ADMINISTRATION ONLY | Due primarily to risk of vein irritation (phlebitis): parenteral nutrition central formula, most chemotherapeutics, calcium chloride, hypertonic saline, epinephrine/dopamine/dobutamine (preferred), and if in small volume [KCl, amiodarone, and quinupristin/dalfopristin (*Synercid*)]. |
| FILTER REQUIRED | PN, lipids (do not use filter < 1.2 micron and *Liposyn* does not require filter), abciximab, some albumin products (*Buminate, Flexbumin*), amiodarone, amphotericin B, diazepam, digoxin immune fab, infliximab, lorazepam, mannitol, phenytoin, propofol (do not use < 5 micron filter)—see IV Drugs chapter in RxPrep Course Book. |

*Images courtesy of Apothecary Products*

# Index